chod'

The Kids' Book of Crosswords

Buster Books

Nacruvalwai

First published in Great Britain in 2011 by Buster Books,
an imprint of Michael O'Mara Books Limited,
9 Lion Yard, Tremadoc Road, London SW4 7NQ
www.mombooks.com/busterbooks

Illustrations and layouts © Buster Books 2011
Puzzles and solutions © Gareth Moore 2011

Illustrations by Sarah Horne

A CIP catalogue record for this book is available from the British Library.

ISBN: 978-1-78055-077-0

2 4 6 8 10 9 7 5 3 1

Papers used by Buster Books are natural, recyclable products
made from wood grown in sustainable forests. The manufacturing processes
conform to the environmental regulations of the country of origin.

Puzzles designed and typeset by Gareth Moore
www.drgarethmoore.com

Cover and layout designed by Barbara Ward

Printed and bound by CPI Group (UK) Ltd,
108 Beddington Lane, Croydon, CR0 4YY, United Kingdom

Contents

Crossword Crazy!

Crosswords are the most popular printed puzzles of all time. They've been around for over 100 years – so your grandparents probably did them when they were children!

The Rules Of Crosswords

The rules of crosswords are very simple: just find the solution word described by each numbered across or down clue and then write it into the corresponding squares in the grid.

Sometimes, you will be able to think of more than one solution to a clue. When this happens, wait until you solve some of the words that cross over that one in the grid, then use these to help you choose the correct solution.

Each clue has a number in brackets at the end, like this: (4). This shows you how many letters are in the word you are trying to guess and matches the number of empty squares in the grid. Occasionally you might see two numbers, like this: (3, 3). This means there are two words to place, each of the given length, such as 'The End'. Don't leave a space between the words in the grid, though – write one letter in each square.

If you see a ';' in a clue, it means the clue is made up of different parts which will help you guess the solution. For example, the clue: 'Opposite of front; rear of your body (4)' provides two clues for 'back'.

The puzzles in this book are divided in to four different sizes, getting harder as you work through the book.

If you get stuck and simply can't find a word and fear you will go crazy, don't despair, all the answers are in the back.

Good luck, and have fun!

Introducing The Puzzle Master, Dr Gareth Moore

Dr Gareth Moore, who created all the puzzles in this book, is an Ace Puzzler, and author of lots of brain-training and puzzle books. These include *Kids' 10-Minute Brain Workout*, *The Kids' Book of Wordsearches*, *The Little Book of Word Searches*, *The Little Book of Crosswords*, *The Little Book of Sudoku Volumes 4 and 5*, *The Brain Workout* and *Train the Brain*.

He writes a monthly magazine called *Sudoku Xtra*, and runs an online puzzle site called PuzzleMix.com. Gareth got a PhD at the University of Cambridge, UK, where he taught machines to recognize the English language.

Level One:

Beginners

Puzzle 1

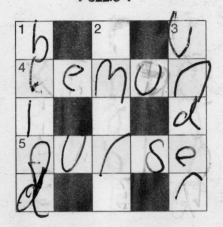

Across

4 Bitter, yellow fruit; a slice of this is sometimes added to cola or other drinks (5)

5 Person trained to look after sick people (5)

Down

1 Unable to see with your eyes (5)

2 Clever; intelligent; brainy (5)

3 Opposite of over; beneath something (5)

Puzzle 2

Across
1 A young deer (4)
3 Small garden creature with a hard shell on its back (5)
4 Easy to break; not strong (4)

Down
1 Wooden panelling surrounding a piece of land (5)
2 Kitchen item used for beating eggs or cream (5)

Puzzle 3

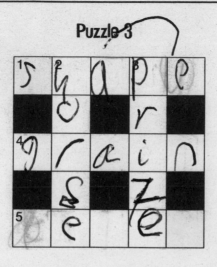

¹S	²h	a	p	e
■	o	■	r	■
⁴g	r	a	i	n
■	s	■	z	■
⁵	e		e	

Across

1 For example: square, triangle, pentagon or circle (5)
4 Hard cereal seed, such as wheat (5)
5 At no time in the past or future (5)

Down

2 Animal that can be ridden (5)
3 Something won in a competition (5)

Puzzle 4

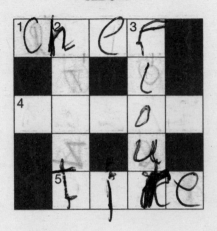

Across
1 Someone who cooks food for you at a restaurant (4)
4 Main or important; high rank in the army (5)
5 Become in need of rest (4)

Down
2 Red playing card (5)
3 Powder used for making bread or cakes (5)

Puzzle 5

Across

1 Thick string, used for tying things up (4)
4 The sharp part of a knife (5)
5 Something opened with a key (4)

Down

1 A red, precious stone; the colour of the slippers in The Wizard of Oz (4)
2 Keyboard instrument with black and white keys (5)
3 The top of a mountain (4)

Puzzle 6

Across
1 A type of light you probably have at home (4)
4 The ability to see; 'eye_____' (5)
5 Not looked after by people, as in 'a ____ animal' (4)

Down
2 Heavenly messenger (5)
3 Container for flowers (3)
4 Plant seeds in the ground (3)

Puzzle 7

Across
2 Run slowly for exercise (3)
4 Foreigner from another planet (5)
5 Greasy substance cut off meat, such as the rind on bacon (3)

Down
1 Teachers in a school or workers in a shop (5)
2 Place where two bones connect (5)
3 Magical being that lives in a lamp and grants wishes (5)

BEGINNERS

Time ....

Puzzle 8

Across

1 The sun, for example; there are lots of these in the night sky (4)

4 Furniture you might eat at (5)

5 Large grassy area where everybody can go and play (4)

Down

2 Walk heavily (5)

3 Used for drawing straight lines (5)

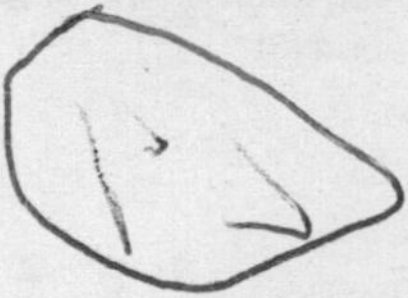

Puzzle 9

Across

1 Choose, as in '____ one of these' (4)
3 Hard, solid rock; a pebble (5)
4 Take part in a game (4)

Down

1 Each separate, coloured part of a flower (5)
2 Sugary sweet (5)

Puzzle 10

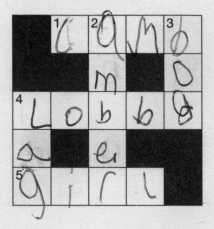

Across
1 Young sheep (4)
4 Entrance hall in a hotel or a block of flats (5)
5 Young woman (4)

Down
2 A yellow gemstone often worn as jewellery (5)
3 Young man (3)
4 Go so slowly you don't keep up with everyone else (3)

Puzzle 11

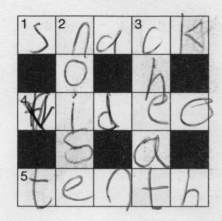

S	N	A	C	K
	O		H	
V	I	D	E	O
	S		A	
T	E	N	T	H

Across
1 A small, quick meal (5)
4 A picture and sound recording (5)
5 The position between ninth and eleventh (5)

Down
2 Loud sound (5)
3 Try to win a game by breaking the rules (5)

Puzzle 12

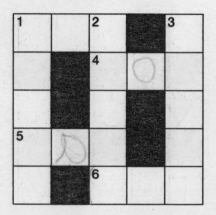

Across

1 Device for plugging multiple electronic devices into (3)

4 Did light, as in 'Yesterday he ___ the candle' (3)

5 The opposite of hello (3)

6 The brightest star in the sky (3)

Down

1 Something you do in your spare time (5)

2 Type of sad jazz music (5)

3 Dirty mark on clothing (5)

Puzzle 13

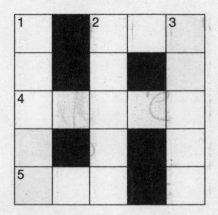

Across

2 A pile of blank paper fastened together in a book (3)

4 Poisoned fruit given to Snow White (5)

5 Cunning and mischievous, as a fox is often described (3)

Down

1 A metal made from copper and zinc; 'as bold as _ _ _ _ _' (5)

2 Young dog (5)

3 An item of clothing worn by women (5)

Puzzle 14

Across
1 Move yourself through water (4)
4 Happy; cheerful (5)
5 When you are in the middle of doing something you are _ _ _ _ (4)

Down
2 The edges of the room that hold up the roof (5)
3 The fifth month of the year (3)
4 Something you have if you go out to work to earn money each day (3)

Puzzle 15

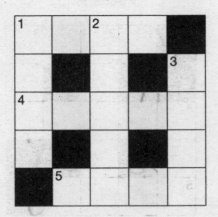

Across
1 Wish someone good ____ for a test (4)
4 Story with a moral, such as those written by Aesop (5)
5 Fix something that is broken (4)

Down
1 Raise up; an elevator (4)
2 Wire for connecting electrical equipment (5)
3 Leash for keeping control of a dog (4)

Puzzle 16

Across

1 Did own, as in 'she ___ that' (3)
4 Move something back and forth against something else, as Aladdin did to make the genie appear (3)
5 A vehicle bigger than a car and suitable for moving things (3)
6 Something used to open locks (3)

Down

1 Weighty; hard to lift (5)
2 You do this when you swallow liquid (5)
3 Prince William married Catherine in Westminster _____ (5)

Puzzle 17

Across

1 Notice that tells you which way to go (4)
3 Two of these on a car windscreen help keep it clean (5)
4 The period from Monday to Sunday (4)

Down

1 You do this to show that you're happy (5)
2 A person from Greece (5)

Puzzle 18

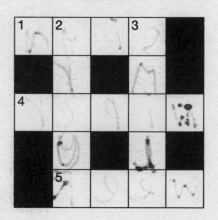

Across
1 Stiff paper, used for crafts (4)
4 Work out a solution, as in
'_ _ _ _ _ a puzzle' (5)
5 A short message or letter; a
musical sound (4)

Down
2 The nut from an oak tree (5)
3 A thick bed covering which
you usually put a cover over
before using (5)

Puzzle 19

Across
1 A young cow (4)
4 A striped orange and black big cat, found in Asia (5)
5 The opposite of shallow (4)

Down
2 Quarrel; disagree (5)
3 Soft covering on a dog or other animal (3)
4 Short word for a toy bear (3)

Puzzle 20

Across
1 Place with exercise equipment (3)
4 The whole number between zero and two (3)
5 Person who treats sick animals (3)
6 Small house or shelter (3)

Down
1 Clothing for a hand used to keep you warm (5)
2 Used for eating and speaking (5)
3 Special meal with lots of food for many people (5)

Puzzle 21

Across
1 Place where a bird sits (5)
4 Draw over something by using another sheet of paper on top (5)
5 Rich, milky topping, sometimes used in coffee or on strawberries and cakes (5)

Down
2 A mistake (5)
3 Chocolate powder (5)

Puzzle 22

Across
1 Succeed at a test or exam (4)
4 Power to do supernatural tricks (5)
5 Not an odd number (4)

Down
2 Surprise; astonish (5)
3 Another name for a pig; a type of flu (5)

Puzzle 23

Across
1 Store a document on a computer (4)
3 Lowest value British coin (5)
4 Thin and graceful (4)

Down
1 Odour (5)
2 Poison from snakes (5)

Puzzle 24

Across

4 Dried plum (5)
5 Strong, aggressive feeling (5)

Down

1 Say words (5)
2 The person who decides who wins in a competition (5)
3 Black and white African horse (5)

Puzzle 25

Across

1 Annoying person; insect that destroys crops (4)
4 Stop for a short while (5)
5 Allow access to (4)

Down

1 Head of the Roman Catholic Church (4)
2 Remains of a tree after it has been cut down (5)
3 Plant with green feathery leaves and fronds (4)

Puzzle 26

Across
1 Opposite of thick (4)
4 A bleeding injury (5)
5 For example: an oak, a sycamore or a fir (4)

Down
2 Building where some families live (5)
3 The opposite to a shake of the head (3)
4 Soaked in water (3)

Puzzle 27

Across
1 Covering worn over the face to hide it (4)
3 Map book (5)
4 Long walk (4)

Down
1 Machine that creates power for vehicles (5)
2 The creature in the Jaws movies (5)

Puzzle 28

Across
1 Noise made by a chicken (5)
4 Something you stick on a letter (5)
5 Wobbly dessert (5)

Down
2 A measure of liquid (5)
3 Desert animal with one or two humps and long eyelashes (5)

Puzzle 29

Across
1 Sunrise (4)
4 Turn around quickly (5)
5 Opposite of right (4)

Down
1 A trip out with a boy- or girlfriend (4)
2 Opposite of black (5)
3 Apartment (4)

Puzzle 30

Across

1. Cut away unwanted parts, for example with scissors (4)
4. Sweet substance, added to many recipes (5)
5. Keen-eyed bird of prey (4)

Down

2. Opposite of smooth (5)
3. Noise made by a cat (5)

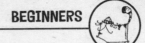

Puzzle 31

Across
1 Quiet; silence (4)
3 Rest on the surface of water;
the opposite of sink (5)
4 Young horse (4)

Down
1 Greeting word (5)
2 Opposite of big (5)

Puzzle 32

Across

1 Thick, flavoured liquid poured on some food, especially meat (5)
4 Cat with streaked fur (5)
5 Metal disc to commemorate an event (5)

Down

2 Not asleep (5)
3 Poisonous snake (5)

Puzzle 33

Across
1 Feeling too pleased with oneself (4)
4 The day before tomorrow (5)
5 Not having any hair (4)

Down
2 Someone who poses for photos (5)
3 Informal word for a man (3)
4 A small round pot; a bath (3)

Puzzle 34

Across
4 Fool someone (5)
5 Move on hands and knees (5)

Down
1 To glue something to something else (5)
2 Essential; absolutely necessary (5)
3 Head bone (5)

Puzzle 35

Across

2 Healthy; strong (3)
4 Reasoned thinking (5)
5 Rest on a chair (3)

Down

1 Instructions you must obey (5)
2 Struggle or argument (5)
3 Sticky (5)

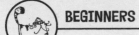

Puzzle 36

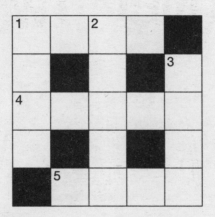

Across
1 Somewhere you store your valuables (4)
4 Not ever (5)
5 Percussion instrument (4)

Down
1 Basin with taps (4)
2 High body temperature (5)
3 Carriage for a baby (4)

Level Two:

Intermediates

Puzzle 37

Across
1 Flickering part of a fire (5)
4 A type of raincoat; a type of computer made by Apple (3)
6 Small, furry animal with a long tail (5)
7 A trail (5)
8 Glide over snow with long metal shoes (3)
9 Drink made from apples (5)

Down
1 Very well known, such as a celebrity (6)
2 Living in water (7)
3 A green jewel (7)
5 Horse chestnut seed (6)

Puzzle 38

Across

1 Warm season that comes between spring and winter (6)
4 Celebration (5)
6 Not clean (5)
8 Decorative cup awarded as a prize (6)

Down

1 Salt water covering a large part of the Earth (3)
2 Person in charge of a town council (5)
3 Answer (5)
4 Colourful liquid used in art (5)
5 TV without pictures? (5)
7 Attempt (3)

Puzzle 39

Across
1 Large, edible fish with pink flesh (6)
4 Useful (7)
6 Leafy, green vegetable that Popeye eats (7)
8 Hang or swing loosely (6)

Down
1 Clean the floor with a broom (5)
2 Part of the body; one circuit of a track (3)
3 A score of nothing in a football match (3)
5 Parent's brother (5)
6 Not happy (3)
7 Pester or repeatedly complain to someone (3)

Puzzle 40

Across

1 Push something down firmly (5)
4 Something a child plays with (3)
5 Turns over and over (5)
6 Add some numbers (3,2)
7 A knight's title, ___ Galahad, for example (3)
8 Deep spoon with long handle, often used to serve soup (5)

Down

1 Ancient Egyptian monument (7)
2 Shadow of the Earth on the moon (7)
3 Female sibling (6)
4 Glittery material used to decorate Christmas trees (6)

Puzzle 41

Across

2 Plan or diagram; a pie or
   bar _ _ _ _ _ (5)
4 Diary to write thoughts in (7)
5 Tap on a door (5)

Down

1 Another word for a soldier or
   fighter (7)
2 Something that tells the time (5)
3 Something trains run on (5)

Puzzle 42

Across

1 Trip to see wild animals in their natural homes (6)
4 Leave behind (7)
5 A difficult task; something that worries you (7)
7 Someone who shoots bows and arrows (6)

Down

1 Large expanse of water between countries (3)
2 Taste (7)
3 Name of one of Santa's reindeers (7)
6 Spoil something (3)

Puzzle 43

Across
2 Superhero's cloak (4)
4 Person who does something brave (4)
5 An army officer of high rank (5)
6 For example: kitchen, lounge or hall (4)
7 Lazy (4)

Down
1 Mythical creature with a woman's body and a fish's tail (7)
2 Perform a magic trick (7)
3 Ancient Egyptian king (7)

Puzzle 44

Across

1 Small, dark red fruit on a stalk with a stone in the centre (6)
4 Long, stringy food served with many Oriental meals (7)
6 Take your clothes off (7)
8 The white surface of teeth (6)

Down

1 Might go on a Queen's head (5)
2 The point where something stops (3)
3 Word for agreeing (3)
5 Stand used by artist to hold a canvas while painting (5)
6 Utilise something (3)
7 Male sheep (3)

Puzzle 45

Across
1 Short version of 'Christmas' (4)
4 For example: drawings, paintings, sculptures and music (3)
6 Grand house (7)
7 Wheel with teeth used in mechanisms (3)
8 Reflection of sound (4)

Down
2 Picture made with small coloured tiles (6)
3 Long tube of minced meat, often served with mash (7)
5 Narrow box for animals to eat from (6)

Puzzle 46

Across

2 Cereal plant used to make flour (5)
4 Male sibling (7)
5 Medium-sized sailing boat (5)

Down

1 Green, leafy salad vegetable (7)
2 Anxiety; something you are concerned about (5)
3 Something you enjoy; a reward (5)

Puzzle 47

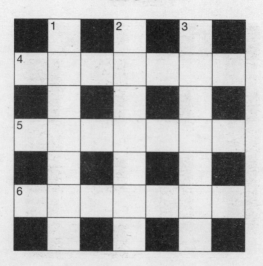

Across

4 Young frog without legs (7)
5 Tool used to tighten bolts (7)
6 Hide (7)

Down

1 Spear used to catch whales (7)
2 Dark green, leafy vegetable (7)
3 Against the law (7)

Puzzle 48

Across

2 Home of Winnie the Pooh, Hundred _ _ _ _ Wood (4)
4 Something you eat (4)
5 Big; sizeable (5)
6 Something a plant grows from (4)
7 Glass part of spectacles (4)

Down

1 Picture made by sticking together scraps of paper (7)
2 Details of where someone lives (7)
3 Official at a football match (7)

Puzzle 49

Across

1 Large, soft feather (5)
4 Solemn promise (3)
6 Living; existing (5)
7 Vegetable that makes you cry (5)
8 Part of the body used for listening (3)
9 Time of day you might see the moon (5)

Down

1 The Black Death, for example (6)
2 Mythical one-horned animal (7)
3 Part of the day just before bedtime (7)
5 Edible nut with a wrinkly surface (6)

Puzzle 50

Across
1. Small animals or insects that carry disease or are harmful to crops (6)
4. Silky material (5)
6. Small juicy fruit containing seeds in its flesh (5)
8. Attractive; nice to look at (6)

Down
1. Stopping at en route, as in 'The train went from London to Southampton ___ Basingstoke' (3)
2. Large country house with grounds (5)
3. Unpleasant; horrible (5)
4. Clever; the opposite of blunt (5)
5. Furniture with legs and a flat top (5)
7. Thin beam of sunlight (3)

Puzzle 51

Across
1 Coldest season of the year (6)
4 Error (7)
6 Waterproof boots (7)
8 A shape or sign that means something (6)

Down
1 Put words on paper (5)
2 The opposite of something, as in 'I will do this but ___ that' (3)
3 Cereal used in bread and biscuits; a famous book called 'The Catcher in the ___' (3)
5 Sit down on your knees (5)
6 Used to be (3)
7 Overhead shot in tennis (3)

Puzzle 52

Across
1 Linked to the universe (6)
4 Write a piece of music (7)
6 Strange; rare (7)
8 A common citrus fruit (6)

Down
1 Circus performer with bright red nose (5)
2 Drink in small quantities (3)
3 Line of text used to prompt an actor (3)
5 A fright (5)
6 Unidentified flying object (abbreviation) (1,1,1)
7 Our closest star (3)

Puzzle 53

Across

1 Fading light in the early evening (4)
3 What you might call a male teacher (3)
5 Spoon used for serving soft food, such as ice cream (5)
6 Sharp cutting tool (5)
7 Utter a word or sentence (3)
8 Not pleasant to look at (4)

Down

1 A heavy disk thrown during athletic events (6)
2 Ghostly; creepy (6)
3 Coiled spiral of metal wire, often found in a mattress (6)
4 Cure for an illness (6)

Puzzle 54

Across

1 Noise made by a duck (5)
5 Person being treated by a doctor (7)
6 Toy with two wheels, which you stand on and power by foot (7)
7 Small garden ornament with beard and pointed hat (5)

Down

2 Standard outfit everyone at the same place wears (7)
3 Decide not to do something; an on-screen button to say 'no' to an option (6)
4 Small type of hawk (6)

Puzzle 55

Across
3 Used for taking photographs (6)
4 In support of (3)
5 Untidy; dirty (5)
7 Male pig (3)
8 Voucher (6)

Down
1 Female horse (4)
2 Wax colouring item (6)
3 Ordinary; usual (6)
6 Outer covering for your foot (4)

Puzzle 56

Across

2 Food selected to help someone become healthier (4)
4 String used to tie up a shoe (4)
5 Fourth month (5)
6 Loose earth (4)
7 Grated peel of a lemon or orange (4)

Down

1 Singing along and following words on a screen (7)
2 Unfreeze (7)
3 To shout or speak suddenly (7)

Puzzle 57

Across

1 Prehistoric animal remains found in rock (6)
4 Precious stone (5)
6 Newly made (5)
8 Sadness (6)

Down

1 Payment; charge (3)
2 Work out a solution (5)
3 Meal at midday (5)
4 Trousers made of denim (5)
5 Thin biscuit (5)
7 Noticed something, as in 'I ___ it happen' (3)

Puzzle 58

Across

1 Instrument often pictured being played by angels (4)
4 Tear something, such as a piece of paper (3)
6 Male who delivers letters (7)
7 Container for storing rubbish (3)
8 Be brave enough to do something (4)

Down

2 Soak up some liquid (6)
3 Imagine something is real (7)
5 Words you address to God (6)

Puzzle 59

Across

4 Machine for carrying people or goods (7)
5 Warm up your muscles before exercise (7)
6 Thin, crispy biscuit (7)

Down

1 The characters that make up the alphabet (7)
2 Absolute quiet (7)
3 Slow-moving mass of ice found on land (7)

Puzzle 60

Across
3 People who catch criminals (6)
4 Female parent (3)
5 A time without war (5)
7 Not strict (3)
8 A light gas used to fill floating
   balloons (6)

Down
1 Tall, rounded roof (4)
2 Loud, shrill cry (6)
3 Doll controlled by hand,
   sometimes with strings (6)
6 A group where people
   enjoy the same hobby;
   black playing card (4)

Puzzle 61

Across
1 Back bones (5)
5 Noise that accompanies lightning (7)
6 Thick, sticky liquid made from sugar (7)
7 Animal kept for wool and meat (5)

Down
2 Food made on Shrove Tuesday (7)
3 Thin piece of metal used for sewing (6)
4 Christian building of worship (6)

Puzzle 62

Across
2 Huge person in fairy tales (5)
4 Difficult; complicated (7)
5 Walk like a soldier (5)

Down
1 Blood-sucking monster (7)
2 Someone who looks after horses (5)
3 What you bite your food with (5)

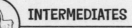

Puzzle 63

Across

1 A rich, moist cake, often topped with cherries (6)
4 Someone who educates you (7)
5 Woman in a play (7)
7 Someone you like and know (6)

Down

1 Instinctive thought: a _ _ _ feeling (3)
2 Vehicle used on farms (7)
3 A sports player (7)
6 Unhappy (3)

Puzzle 64

Across
1 Well known (6)
4 Place to catch a train (7)
6 Speak secretively (7)
8 Fantasy fire-breathing
   beast (6)

Down
1 Go and bring (5)
2 Came across someone (3)
3 Male child (3)
5 Large sea (5)
6 Marry someone (3)
7 To drop or sink to a lower
   level (3)

Puzzle 65

Across
2 Cow's meat (4)
4 Group two things together (4)
5 Complete; absolute (5)
6 Often goes with pepper (4)
7 Traditional story about gods and heroes (4)

Down
1 First month of the year (7)
2 From Great Britain (7)
3 A green precious stone (7)

Puzzle 66

Across
1 Male parent (6)
4 White granules sometimes added to sweeten tea or coffee (5)
6 Each one; all of something (5)
8 Opening in a wall, usually filled with glass (6)

Down
1 Short for 'influenza' (3)
2 For example, Black Beauty (5)
3 To answer someone (5)
4 Long, narrow tube for drinking (5)
5 Colour for 'go' (5)
7 Use oars to move a boat (3)

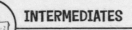

Puzzle 67

Across
2 Rub out (5)
4 Soldiers on horses (7)
5 Rope for leading a dog (5)

Down
1 Holiday vehicle for camping (7)
2 Electronic mail (5)
3 Our planet (5)

Puzzle 68

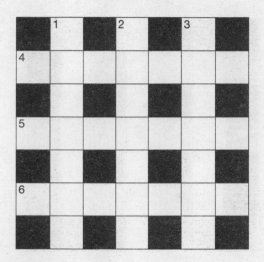

Across
4 This evening (7)
5 Gentle rain (7)
6 Red, orange, yellow, green, blue, indigo and violet (7)

Down
1 Small carpet for wiping your feet on (7)
2 Making lots of small bubbles (7)
3 Opposite of deep (7)

Puzzle 69

Across

2 Notice board; in astrology, which star _ _ _ _ are you? (4)
4 A walking track (4)
5 The overall amount (5)
6 Organ used for breathing (4)
7 Very tall plant with branches and leaves (4)

Down

1 Big black leopard (7)
2 Vehicle travelling back and forth (7)
3 A wreath of flowers worn around the neck or hung up (7)

Puzzle 70

Across

1 On time; without delay (6)
4 Opposite of light (5)
6 Before all the others (5)
8 Primary painting colour (6)

Down

1 Mince ___, eaten at Christmas (3)
2 Person in charge of a town who wears a gold chain (5)
3 Grilled bread (5)
4 Cheery; contented (5)
5 Very bad (5)
7 Female pig (3)

Puzzle 71

Across
3 Soft floor covering (6)
4 Reddish, dog-like animal (3)
5 Small fairy (5)
7 Opposite of wet (3)
8 Something you must keep to yourself (6)

Down
1 A cab (4)
2 Large area of dry land, often covered in sand (6)
3 Red-brown metal used in wires (6)
6 Thought (4)

Puzzle 72

Across

1 Instructions for cooking food (6)
4 Greet on arrival (7)
5 Unusual; different (7)
7 Long-stemmed, crunchy green vegetable, often eaten raw (6)

Down

1 Not cooked (3)
2 School for continuing education (7)
3 Say that you will definitely do something (7)
6 Produce an egg, if you're a hen (3)

Puzzle 73

Across
1 To handle a situation (4)
3 Said to someone when you leave them (3)
5 Woolly animal, like a smaller camel without a hump (5)
6 Joint of your arm (5)
7 For example: brazil, hazel, almond (3)
8 Pull something heavy (4)

Down
1 Pillar, often found in Greek and Roman ruins (6)
2 For example: Earth, Jupiter or Mars (6)
3 Hairdresser for men (6)
4 Small crawling insect with pincers (6)

Puzzle 74

		A	N	G	E	Y
	P				A	
T	O	U	R	I	S	T
	L				T	
G	L	A	S	S	E	S
	E				R	
A	N	G	L	E		

Across
1 Not very happy (5)
5 Someone who visits places abroad (7)
6 Spectacles (7)
7 The measurement between two lines that meet at a point (5)

Down
2 Light umbrella used in the sunshine (7)
3 Christian festival during spring (6)
4 Powder inside a flower (6)

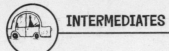

Puzzle 75

Across

3 About the sea; name for a soldier serving on board a ship (6)

4 Object used to cool yourself (3)

5 Raised platform for theatre shows (5)

7 Covered in ice (3)

8 The opposite of arrive (6)

Down

1 Feel you would like something, as in 'I _ _ _ _ this' (4)

2 Small creature with six legs (6)

3 Man in charge (6)

6 Female child (4)

Puzzle 76

Across

2 Circular device found on cars (5)

4 Something old and valuable (7)

5 Time when you are young; type of club for young people (5)

Down

1 Not funny (7)

2 Blustery, as in 'this is _ _ _ _ _ weather' (5)

3 Giggle (5)

Puzzle 77

Across
1 From France (6)
4 Glasses worn for swimming (7)
6 Something that is difficult to solve (7)
8 Not anyone (6)

Down
1 What you walk on (5)
2 Object laid by birds, fish, reptiles and insects (3)
3 Owns (3)
5 A person who is against you (5)
6 Metal fastening (3)
7 Shout disapproval (3)

Puzzle 78

Across
1 Small mark (4)
4 Found at the top of the thigh; the fruit of a rose (3)
6 Remove clothing (7)
7 Slice with a knife (3)
8 Yellow part of an egg (4)

Down
2 Meal packed to eat outside, such as in the park (6)
3 Needing a drink (7)
5 Chalk crayon (6)

Puzzle 79

Across
1 Jar for holding flowers (4)
3 Flying night-time animal (3)
5 Delicate pottery (5)
6 Pale (5)
7 In the middle of (3)
8 Not costing anything (4)

Down
1 _ _ _ _ _ _ cleaner, used for hoovering (6)
2 Protection carried by a soldier (6)
3 Nocturnal black and white animal (6)
4 Sea animal with a hard shell on its back (6)

Puzzle 80

Across
1 The opposite of full (5)
5 A gift from someone (7)
6 Belonging to the same family (7)
7 A room used for writing and reading (5)

Down
2 Hot-tasting yellow food paste, often added to ham (7)
3 Glittery material used to decorate Christmas trees (6)
4 Religious leader (6)

Puzzle 81

Across

2 Cut shorter (4)
4 Market (4)
5 Vegetable that makes you cry; a crisp flavour, 'cheese and _____' (5)
6 The opposite direction to West (4)
7 Fast, graceful animal with antlers (4)

Down

1 Light-weight waterproof coat (7)
2 Sports shoe with rubber sole (7)
3 Sickness (7)

Puzzle 82

Across
1 Plant on which grapes grow (4)
4 To be able; 'I _ _ _ do this' (3)
6 Large bird that eats flesh from dead animals (7)
7 Opposite of 'no' (3)
8 Shout loudly (4)

Down
2 Harm done to someone (6)
3 Great joy; intense emotion (7)
5 Everyday; regular (6)

Puzzle 83

Across

2 Board game with kings, queens and pawns (5)
4 Damage; ruin something (7)
5 Doctor's assistant (5)

Down

1 One hundred years (7)
2 Tidy up; neaten (5)
3 A small piece of rock (5)

Puzzle 84

Across

1 Large bird that gobbles (6)
4 Large bird with pouch in beak for holding fish (7)
5 Ancient Egyptian king (7)
7 Envelope contents (6)

Down

1 Hit something gently (3)
2 Let go of something (7)
3 Put a magic spell on someone; delight someone (7)
6 Belonging to the woman or girl (3)

Puzzle 85

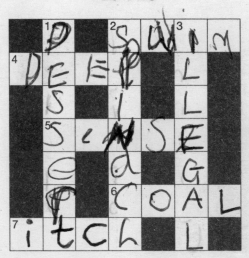

Across

2 Travel through water using your hands and feet (4)

4 A long way down, especially under water (4)

5 For example: sight, hearing, touch, taste or smell (5)

6 Black substance mined and used for fuel (4)

7 Scratch (4)

Down

1 Pudding (7)

2 Leafy, dark green vegetable (7)

3 Unlawful; forbidden (7)

Puzzle 86

Across

1 Secret plan to do something bad (4)
4 An obligation to repay something (3)
6 Girl's bag for carrying a purse (7)
7 When something is expected to arrive it is '___'; need to be paid (3)
8 Small loaf of bread (4)

Down

2 Small, four-legged reptile with a long tail (6)
3 Young child who has started to walk (7)
5 The white surface of teeth (6)

Puzzle 87

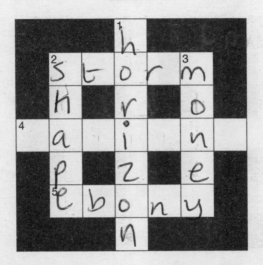

Across
2 Bad weather with thunder and lightning (5)
4 Brave; courageous (7)
5 Hard black wood, sometimes used for piano keys (5)

Down
1 Line where the sky meets the Earth (7)
2 Outline of something; a square, circle and triangle are all types of _ _ _ _ _ (5)
3 Coins or notes used to buy things (5)

Puzzle 88

Across
4 Official at a football match (7)
5 Badly behaved (7)
6 Young goose (7)

Down
1 Shape with six sides (7)
2 Common white or grey seabird (7)
3 Fate (7)

 **INTERMEDIATES** Time ....

Puzzle 89

Across
2 Thin layer covering a surface (4)
4 Mix with a spoon (4)
5 Do very well at something (5)
6 The bottom of your ear (4)
7 Hard clothing you put on your foot (4)

Down
1 Warm up your muscles before exercise (7)
2 Small, brown mark on skin (7)
3 Bedtime song for babies (7)

Puzzle 90

Across
1 On a ship (6)
4 Entertain someone (5)
6 Book for keeping day-by-day notes of what someone does (5)
8 Scottish cloth with coloured patterns (6)

Down
1 A goal or target (3)
2 Where sports events take place (5)
3 Place where milk is processed (5)
4 No longer a child (5)
5 Beneath; below (5)
7 Move quickly on foot (3)

Puzzle 91

Across
1 Area around the North Pole (6)
4 Shopkeeper selling flowers (7)
6 Clothing worn in bed (7)
8 Planted ground around a house (6)

Down
1 Narrow street or passage (5)
2 Motor vehicle (3)
3 Feline animal (3)
5 A mark on clothes (5)
6 Farm animal with a snout and a curly tail (3)
7 If you cut yourself, you may need first ___ (3)

Puzzle 92

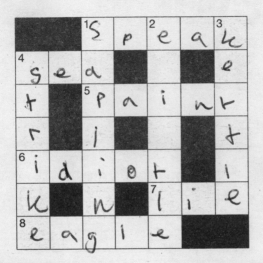

Across

1 Talk; say something (5)
4 Large expanse of water between countries (3)
5 Liquid put on walls to decorate (5)
6 Foolish person (5)
7 Say something that isn't true (3)
8 Large bird of prey (5)

Down

1 Young tree (7)
2 Biblical letter (7)
3 Device for boiling water (6)
4 Light a match (6)

Level Three:

Advanced

Puzzle 93

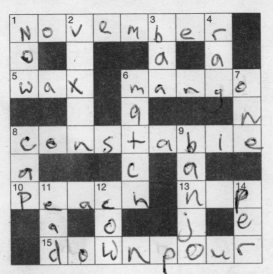

The filled-in crossword grid:

Row 1: N O V E M B E R
Row 2: O (down) . . . . a . a
Row 3: W A X . M A N G O
Row 4: . . . . q . . . n
Row 5: C O N S T A B L E
Row 6: a . . . c . a . .
Row 7: P E A C H . n P
Row 8: a . o . j . e
Row 9: D O W N P O U R

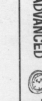

Across
1 Eleventh month (8)
5 Substance used for making crayons and candles (3)
6 Juicy tropical fruit (5)
8 Police officer (9)
10 Pinkish-yellow juicy fruit with furry skin (5)
13 Bite sharply, like a dog might do (3)
15 Heavy fall of rain (8)

Down
1 At this time (3)
2 Female fox (5)
3 Sound made by a sheep (3)
4 Old piece of cloth (3)
6 Small stick struck to create a flame (5)
7 A single item (3)
8 Soft, flat hat (3)
9 Long-necked musical instrument with strings to pluck (5)
11 A Muslim festival (3)
12 Farmyard animal that produces milk (3)
14 For each, as in 'one ___ person' (3)

ADVANCED

Time

Across
4 Warning sound (5)
6 Piece of writing with rhyming lines (4)
7 Gang or crowd who are hard to control (3)
9 Wicked person, especially in a story (7)
10 Playing card '1' (3)
12 Glass part of a telescope or spectacles (4)
13 Copy a picture by drawing over it on thin paper (5)

Down
1 Bet money on something (6)
2 Between your shoulder and your hand (3)
3 Criminal in prison (7)
5 First part of the day (7)
8 Large, wooden hammer (6)
11 Do something wrongly (3)

Puzzle 95

Across

1 Get pleasure from (5)
3 The cover over a building (4)
5 Hover in the air (5)
8 Someone who travels in a spaceship (9)
9 Sharp point growing on a rose stem (5)
11 Noise made by a clock (4)
12 Opposite of loud (5)

Down

1 Small mischievous fairy (3)
2 Whirlwind (7)
4 Something that is true (4)
6 Large bird that can run fast but can't fly (7)
7 Edible freshwater fish (5)
8 Parent's sister (4)
10 Something used to catch fish with (3)

ADVANCED

Time

Across
1 What comes out when you turn the tap on (5)
4 Weapon for shooting arrows (3)
6 High-ranking teacher (9)
7 Plant used for food, some of which are also called 'greens' (9)
10 A joke based on multiple meanings of words (3)
11 Someone who flies an aeroplane (5)

Down
1 Cry (4)
2 Sledge for sliding downhill (8)
3 Competition to arrive first (4)
4 Popular American ball game similar to Rounders (8)
5 Period of fighting between armies (3)
7 Very important person (abbreviation) (1,1,1)
8 Short journey (4)
9 Change (4)

Across

1 Word used to introduce a contrasting viewpoint (3)
3 Real or correct (4)
5 The pink flesh around your teeth (3)
6 Small mug for tea (3)
8 Real-life picture (5)
9 The length of time that a person has been alive (3)
10 Short sleep (3)
11 Hard; not easy to bend (5)
13 Warm (3)
15 Climbing evergreen plant, often grows up buildings (3)
17 Story (4)
18 The cat sat on the _ _ _ (3)

Down

1 Creepy-crawly (3)
2 Violent storm (7)
3 Group of three people (4)
4 Large, Australian, flightless bird (3)
6 Agree with (7)
7 Small seed found in fruit (3)
9 The blackened remains of a fire (3)
12 A small island (4)
14 Not in (3)
16 So far; up until now (3)

Across

1 Last month of the year (8)
5 Loud noise (3)
6 Incorrect (5)
8 Exactly the same (9)
10 Soil; ground (5)
13 Having lived for a long time (3)
15 Someone who looks after sheep (8)

Down

1 Disc with a film or TV show on it (abbreviation) (1,1,1)
2 Small boat with a paddle (5)
3 A metal pole (3)
4 Did go for a run (3)
6 Look at a television set (5)
7 Substance for styling hair (3)
8 Frozen water (3)
9 Shut something (5)
11 A donkey (3)
12 Definite article; a particular item, as in 'I want _ _ _ one over there' (3)
14 Past tense of 'do', as in 'what I _ _ _ yesterday' (3)

ADVANCED

 Time ....

Across
1 Opposite of white (5)
3 Measurement used in the USA as a small measure of length (4)
5 Come into flower (5)
8 Washing powder (9)
9 Home for a rabbit (5)
11 Part of your body used for walking on (4)
12 Land for growing crops (5)

Down
1 Float gently up and down in water (3)
2 Really old (7)
4 Clue (4)
6 Halloween month (7)
7 Third month (5)
8 Unable to hear (4)
10 Did own (3)

ADVANCED

Time ....

Across

1 Thin paper used for blowing your nose (6)
4 Thick black liquid used for surfacing roads (3)
5 Mark left after an injury has healed (4)
7 Sorrow; misfortune (3)
10 Large country house, especially in Roman times (5)
11 Make an offer in an auction (3)
13 Join two things together (4)
16 The edge of a hole; part of your mouth (3)
17 Bicycle for two people (6)

Down

1 Have a go at an activity (3)
2 Urgent call for help (abbreviation) (1,1,1)
3 Small job; chore (6)
4 An even number just less than three (3)
6 Sideways-walking shellfish with pincers and legs (4)
7 Case to carry money in (6)
8 Whole numbers are either ____ or odd (4)
9 Airborne insect (3)
12 Mischievous pixie (3)
14 Tease; a child (3)
15 Tall tree with broad leaves (3)

Puzzle 101

ADVANCED Time ......

Across

1 Foolish (5)
4 Place where adults buy drinks (3)
6 Say sorry (9)
7 Type of music composed by Mozart (9)
10 Fasten; ___ your shoelaces (3)
11 Unpleasant; horrible (5)

Down

1 Long, soft seat for more than one person (4)
2 Flavoured fruit drink (8)
3 Round toy that goes up and down on a string (2-2)
4 Daughter of a king and queen (8)
5 Pollinating insect (3)
7 Baby's bed (3)
8 Graceful white water bird (4)
9 Woman (4)

Across
4 Common; ordinary (5)
6 A light-brown colour (4)
7 Ask people in the street to give you money (3)
9 The gathering of crops (7)
10 Wheel with teeth used in mechanisms (3)
12 Large farm building used for storage (4)
13 Book containing a story (5)

Down
1 Wanting food (6)
2 Poke (3)
3 Styles of clothes that people like (7)
5 The characters that make up the alphabet (7)
8 Small, rounded stone (6)
11 Obtained (3)

Puzzle 103

ADVANCED

Time ....

Across

1 Great happiness (3)
3 Choose something (3)
5 What we breathe (3)
7 TV company, 'British Broadcasting Corporation' (abbreviation) (1,1,1)
8 Avoid (5)
10 Colourfully-winged insect (9)
13 Problem with a computer program (5)
16 You must ___ and drink to stay alive (3)
18 Belonging to us (3)
19 Father (3)
20 The person I am talking to (3)

Down

1 Work done for money (3)
2 Medium-sized sailing boat (5)
3 A rock with metal in it (3)
4 Hot, brewed drink (3)
6 To a great amount, as in 'she was ____ happy' (4)
9 Video cassette recorder (abbreviation) (1,1,1)
10 Meat of a cow (4)
11 Also; as well (3)
12 Full of flames (5)
14 Discard something unwanted (3)
15 A long thin stick, such as one used for fishing (3)
17 Abbreviation for the day after Wednesday (3)

Time ......

Across

1 What can be seen right now (4)
4 Stop living (3)
5 Sound made by a cow (3)
6 Liquid used for writing (3)
8 Frequently (5)
9 The closing to a story, 'The ___' (3)
10 The closest star to Earth (3)
11 Liquid unit (5)
13 Try to get money from someone through a legal process (3)
15 Fish's eggs (3)
16 A group of objects belonging together (3)
17 Small water lizard (4)

Down

1 Underwear worn on your top half to keep you warm (4)
2 Came first in a race (3)
3 Glowing remains of a fire (6)
4 Quick sketch or drawing (6)
6 Put in (6)
7 House for a dog (6)
12 Check something (4)
14 Tall, rounded vase (3)

ADVANCED ◷ Time ....

Across
1 Shape associated with love (5)
3 Liquid food often made with vegetables and cream (4)
5 Strip of material worn around the neck to keep you warm (5)
8 Jam made with oranges (9)
9 Tap on a door (5)
11 Become in need of rest (4)
12 Elephants' tusks are made of this (5)

Down
1 Male equivalent of 'her' (3)
2 Mountain that erupts with molten lava (7)
4 Free of contamination (4)
6 Place where aeroplanes take off and land (7)
7 Container for keeping drinks hot or cold (5)
8 Watery ditch surrounding a castle (4)
10 Button on a computer (3)

ADVANCED

Time

Across
1 Disgraceful (8)
5 For example: brazil, hazel, almond (3)
6 Sound made by a horse (5)
8 Fierce storm with strong winds (9)
10 Without anything missing (5)
13 Perform on stage (3)
15 The way in to a place (8)

Down
1 Break a law, especially a religious one (3)
2 Raised table in a church (5)
3 The cost for something (3)
4 Carry or drag something heavy (3)
6 Unpleasant sound (5)
7 Tool used for scraping up weeds (3)
8 In what way? (3)
9 Once more (5)
11 Tint; colour (3)
12 Large number (3)
14 Abbreviation for the day after Monday (3)

Puzzle 107

Across

1 Picture painted on the wall (5)
4 Narrow end of something (3)
6 Model of a person used to scare birds away from crops (9)
7 Time between morning and evening (9)
10 Short for et cetera; 'and other things like this' (3)
11 The crime of stealing (5)

Down

1 Untidy state (4)
2 To do with love (8)
3 Similar to (4)
4 Slow creature with a shell (8)
5 Animal's foot (3)
7 Wonder (3)
8 Part of a plant that grows in the ground (4)
9 A bird's home (4)

Time

Across
4 Room under the roof of a house (5)
6 Green part of tree foliage (4)
7 Something a child plays with (3)
9 Yellow root vegetable (7)
10 Noah's ship for pairs of animals (3)
12 Snake noise (4)
13 Party where people dance (5)

Down
1 Trip to see wild animals in their natural homes (6)
2 A small part of something (3)
3 African big cat with spotted coat (7)
5 Decayed grass and leaves used to help plants grow (7)
8 Used to stop a boat from moving (6)
11 Family; relatives (3)

Across

1 Tall tree with shiny bark (5)
3 Cover something in paper (4)
5 Girl's outfit (5)
8 Ninth month (9)
9 Sit down on your knees (5)
11 Poke or jab someone (4)
12 Powdery ice on the ground (5)

Down

1 Opposite of good (3)
2 Shake with fear (7)
4 Fruit grown on trees, narrower near the stalk (4)
6 For example: Julius Caesar or Augustus (7)
7 Thick slice of meat (5)
8 Cleaning substance (4)
10 Allow someone to do something (3)

Across

1 Coloured part of the eye (4)

4 Evergreen tree with needle-like leaves (4)

7 Green citrus fruit, sometimes added to drinks (4)

8 Melody (4)

9 Spotty mushroom (9)

12 Fail to hit (4)

14 A large measure of land (4)

16 Cereal plant used for porridge (4)

17 A gap in something, such as clothing (4)

Down

1 Sick; not well (3)

2 How fast something moves (5)

3 Small, crawling insect (3)

5 Currency used in many European countries (4)

6 Basic unit of a living organism (4)

9 When describing animals, _ _ _ _ is the opposite of 'wild' (4)

10 This as well; too (4)

11 Rubbish (5)

13 Tool with sharp teeth for cutting wood (3)

15 Two of these are used when you look at the world (3)

Puzzle 111

Across

1 A repeated visual design (7)
6 Snake-shaped fish (3)
7 Christmas hymn (5)
8 Very tall flower with big yellow petals (9)
10 Time of day when you might see the moon (5)
12 Male equivalent of daughter (3)
13 Old-fashioned word for a snake (7)

Down

1 Colourful country bird with a long tail (8)
2 Strong claw, often found on a bird (5)
3 Often used to get from one floor to another in a shopping mall (9)
4 And not, as in 'neither this ___ that' (3)
5 Woodwind instrument (8)
9 Rubbish (5)
11 For example: oxygen or hydrogen (3)

Across
1 Theatre show with sung music (5)
3 Stretched tight (4)
5 Sudden, bright light (5)
8 U-shaped piece of metal for a horse's hoof (9)
9 Let someone do something; permit (5)
11 Bucket (4)
12 Mix of yellow and blue (5)

Down
1 When I leave the house I set _ _ _ (3)
2 Type of school bag (7)
4 Large plant with a trunk (4)
6 Post sent around the world by aeroplane (7)
7 Wild, wolf-like animal with wicked laugh (5)
8 Shout this to appeal for assistance (4)
10 Success; victory (3)

ADVANCED  Time _____

Across

1 Not quick (4)
4 Available for business, especially if a shop (4)
7 A _ _ _ _ of shoes (4)
8 Something that you play (4)
9 Soft, cuddly toy (5,4)
12 For example: kitchen, lounge or hall (4)
14 For example: Henry VIII (4)
16 Law (4)
17 Boat made of logs tied together (4)

Down

1 Juice inside a tree (3)
2 The Earth and all its people (5)
3 Small barrel (3)
5 What a person is called (4)
6 Period of 365 days (4)
9 Pie containing jam (4)
10 Building entrance (4)
11 Someone who makes bread and cakes (5)
13 A big cup (3)
15 Remove insides from dead fish or animals (3)

ADVANCED

Time

Across

4 Agreeable sounds made by instruments and voices (5)
6 Slightly wet (4)
7 Put money on the result of a game (3)
9 Dried grape; fruit used in a sweet bun (7)
10 A small wound (3)
12 Move in a circular direction (4)
13 Film seen at the cinema (5)

Down

1 Group of countries ruled by one person or country (6)
2 Metal point on a pen (3)
3 Milk contains _ _ _ _ _ _ _, which is good for bones and teeth (7)
5 One hundred years (7)
8 Person who serves food in a restaurant (6)
11 Heavy unit of weight (3)

Across

1 School work you do at home (8)

5 Playground game where one person chases the rest (3)

6 Cleaning material (5)

8 A folding chair that you might take to the beach (9)

10 Fruit used for making wine (5)

13 Blockade across a river (3)

15 Felt curious about something (8)

Down

1 Covering for the head (3)

2 Tricks done by a performer to impress people (5)

3 Bird that calls 'too-wit too-woo' (3)

4 Clothes for sports (3)

6 Ride on a bicycle (5)

7 Female equivalent of 'his' (3)

8 Common family pet (3)

9 Small, poisonous snake (5)

11 A straight line of people (3)

12 Metal dish with a handle used for cooking (3)

14 Crazy; not sane (3)

ADVANCED

Time

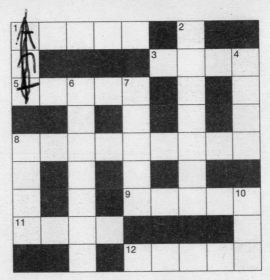

Across

1 Very small person (5)
3 Hard foot of a horse (4)
5 Newspapers and television in general (5)
8 White Arctic bear (5,4)
9 More than usual (5)
11 Place where a wild animal lives (4)
12 You dry your face or hands with this (5)

Down

1 Faintly lit (3)
2 Gather (7)
4 Number of sides a rectangle has (4)
6 Friendly sea animal with a fin (7)
7 Think the same as someone else (5)
8 Move something towards you (4)
10 The whole quantity of something (3)

Puzzle 117

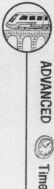

ADVANCED

Time ....

Across

1 Bumper car (6)
4 A gorilla, for example (3)
5 Added to (4)
7 Jump on one foot (3)
10 Clothing worn over the front of the body to protect clothes (5)
11 Home decorating (1,1,1)
13 Have to, as in 'you ____ do this' (4)
16 How something is done (3)
17 Hair accessory (6)

Down

1 Wild animal's home (3)
2 Briefly place something into a liquid and then take it back out (3)
3 Great unhappiness (6)
4 In the past; long ___ (3)
6 Country (4)
7 Tool for putting in nails (6)
8 Ticket in or out of a place (4)
9 Shed tears (3)
12 Slippery and cold (3)
14 Small flap used to mark a page (3)
15 Belonging to you (3)

ADVANCED

Time

Across

4 Sudden feeling of fear (5)
6 Thin metal sheet used for cooking (4)
7 Cardboard container (3)
9 Small falcon (7)
10 Stitch together with a needle and thread (3)
12 Write your signature (4)
13 The main part of your body (5)

Down

1 If you jump into a swimming pool, you will make a _ _ _ _ _ _ (6)
2 Tell a lie (3)
3 Small book with paper covers (7)
5 A picture made by sticking scraps of paper together (7)
8 Jail (6)
11 Deep frying pan used to make Chinese food (3)

Puzzle 119

Across

1 Slightly open (4)
3 Mixture of smoke and fog (4)
5 Short hairs on a man's chin (7)
9 Rules of a country (3)
10 Stand used by artists for a painting (5)
11 To be able; 'I _ _ _ do this' (3)
12 Itch with fingernails (7)
16 Give food to a person (4)
17 Connects devices to electricity (4)

Down

1 The horns on a deer (7)
2 Rodent that resembles a large mouse (3)
3 Cry uncontrollably (3)
4 Thick liquid used for cooking (3)
5 Make a promise (5)
6 Anxious; worried (5)
7 Burp (5)
8 Time when the sun sets (7)
13 Stick used to play pool or billiards (3)
14 A joining word, as in 'this _ _ _ that' (3)
15 Slang term for a police officer (3)

ADVANCED

Time

Across

1 Small bird with a short, thick beak (5)
3 Repeatedly hit the palms of your hands together (4)
5 What you turn to steer a vehicle (5)
8 Every person (9)
9 Large vehicle for moving goods (5)
11 Long, pointed tooth of an elephant (4)
12 Taking a short time (5)

Down

1 More than one but less than several (3)
2 Taste (7)
4 Small horse (4)
6 Short hair on your eyelid (7)
7 Faithful (5)
8 The way out (4)
10 Long-haired ox (3)

Puzzle 121

Across

1 Hard covering over a healing cut or graze (4)

4 Uncut bread (4)

7 Hair on the neck of a horse or lion (4)

8 Primary painting colour (4)

9 Rough paper used to smooth wood (9)

12 Specific day in history when something happened (4)

14 Hold on to (4)

16 Bad or wicked (4)

17 The direction in which the sun rises (4)

Down

1 The result of adding some numbers (3)

2 Mix together smoothly (5)

3 Taxi (3)

5 Turn over quickly (4)

6 For example: grizzly, polar or teddy (4)

9 Another word for 'team' in football (4)

10 Something you write to help you remember things (4)

11 Joint connecting your leg to your foot (5)

13 Evening before an important day (3)

15 Place something somewhere (3)

Across

1 A pale colour (6)

4 A long way (3)

5 Something designed to catch you out (4)

7 To and ___; going backwards and forwards (3)

10 The colour of earth (5)

11 Space between two things (3)

13 A plant growing where it isn't wanted (4)

16 Large tree with acorns (3)

17 The magician pulled a _____ out of his hat! (6)

Down

1 Be nosy (3)

2 Took a seat (3)

3 Small, portable computer (6)

4 On behalf of (3)

6 Finger jewellery (4)

7 Colourful part of a plant (6)

8 Woodwind instrument (4)

9 Place where wild animals are kept for people to see (3)

12 Question someone (3)

14 Touch gently with a tissue in order to clean or dry (3)

15 Note down quickly (3)

Puzzle 123

Across
4 Book of maps (5)
6 Melt from frozen (4)
7 Joined someone at an agreed place (3)
9 Chief law officer in US counties (7)
10 Shown where to go (3)
12 Cage or house for chickens (4)
13 To do with kings and queens (5)

Down
1 Solicitor; expert in legal matters (6)
2 Tropical vegetable, like a potato (3)
3 Hair on an animal's face (7)
5 Edible fish or shellfish (7)
8 Perfectly-round shape (6)
11 Female deer (3)

Time

Across

1 Pack things tightly into a space (3)

3 Place where scientists work (3)

5 I am, he is, you ___ (3)

7 Look unusually pale or ill (3)

8 Fame; honour (5)

10 Flying vehicle with wings and an engine (9)

13 Useful (5)

16 Small container for food (3)

18 Tool for chopping wood (3)

19 Bite sharply, like a dog might do (3)

20 Colour of a stop light (3)

Down

1 Lower, movable part of the face (3)

2 Large country house with grounds (5)

3 Part of the body between the feet and the hips (3)

4 Noise made by a ghost (3)

6 Ancient instrument, like a small harp (4)

9 Text speak for 'laughing out loud' (abbreviation) (1,1,1)

10 A steady pain (4)

11 Opposite of even (3)

12 Make a change (5)

14 Religious woman (3)

15 Small barking sound (3)

17 Something you sleep on (3)

Puzzle 125

Across
1 Opposite of stale (5)
4 Gave food to (3)
6 Spying; the use of spies (9)
7 Dark-coloured songbird (9)
10 Fetch; obtain (3)
11 Opposite of long (5)

Down
1 Something that is burning is on _ _ _ _ (4)
2 Large, grey animal with big ears and a trunk (8)
3 Person who does something brave (4)
4 Pink wading bird (8)
5 Planned for a certain time (3)
7 Larger than normal size (3)
8 Lovingly touch someone with your lips (4)
9 Special food programme; it's important to eat a balanced _ _ _ _ (4)

Time

Across

1 Yellow food made from almonds and sugar (8)
5 Pester or repeatedly complain to someone (3)
6 Father Christmas (5)
8 Tried (9)
10 To march, long and far (5)
13 Highest part of something (3)
15 A one-floor house (8)

Down

1 Grown-up male person (3)
2 Opposite of left (5)
3 Small round green vegetable that grows in a pod (3)
4 The opposite of something, as in 'I will do this but ___ that' (3)
6 To summarize something (3,2)
7 The opposite of 'subtract' (3)
8 Appropriate; suitable (3)
9 The result of adding up some numbers (5)
11 Steal something (3)
12 Plural of 'man' (3)
14 Wooden bench in a church (3)

ADVANCED   Time _____

Across

4 Special prize given for achievement (5)

6 Large shellfish with two shells of equal size (4)

7 The number of fingers and thumbs you have (3)

9 Whirlwind (7)

10 For each, as in 'one ___ person' (3)

12 Joy; delight (4)

13 In the countryside (5)

Down

1 Photo-taking device (6)

2 For example: drawings, paintings, sculptures and music (3)

3 Shiny, powdery substance used in crafts (7)

5 Loving; loyal (7)

8 Twist string together (6)

11 What Aladdin did to the lamp (3)

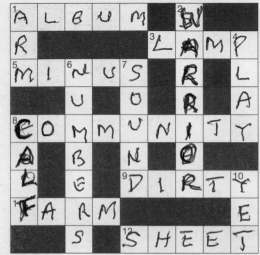

The completed crossword grid contains:

A	L	B	U	M		A			
R					L	A	M	P	
M	I	N	U	S		R		L	
		U		O		R		A	
C	O	M	M	U	N	I	T	Y	
A		B		N		O			
L		E			D	I	R	T	Y
F	A	R	M						E
		S			S	H	E	E	T

Across

1 Book for collecting photos or stamps (5)
3 Illuminates a room (4)
5 Symbol used to indicate subtraction (5)
8 Group of people living in one place (9)
9 Not clean (5)
11 Place where pigs and cows are often kept (4)
12 Piece of paper (5)

Down

1 Limb connected to your shoulder (3)
2 Someone who fights in battle (7)
4 A theatre show (4)
6 1, 2 and 3 are _ _ _ _ _ _ _ (7)
7 Something you can hear (5)
8 A part of your leg, below the knee (4)
10 It hasn't happened _ _ _ (3)

ADVANCED

Time ....

Across
1 White bony parts in your mouth (5)
4 Large piece of wood from a fallen tree (3)
6 A way to cook eggs (9)
7 Mark left by a step (9)
10 Opposite of no (3)
11 Someone taught by a teacher (5)

Down
1 Something children play with (4)
2 Very big (8)
3 Hurt or damage someone (4)
4 Hard candy on a stick (8)
5 Deity; a being that is worshipped (3)
7 Cook in hot fat (3)
8 Object used on stage in a theatre (4)
9 Work hard (4)

Time

Across

1 Deep breath of relief or sadness (4)
4 Make changes (4)
7 British nobleman (4)
8 Medicine (4)
9 Instrument often used to play jazz (9)
12 Level; smooth (4)
14 Young sheep; Mary had a little ____ (4)
16 Large piece of material on a ship, used to catch the wind (4)
17 Indian style of meditation (4)

Down

1 Look at something with your eyes (3)
2 Opposite of goodbye (5)
3 Child (3)
5 Group of three people (4)
6 Large, cruel giant (4)
9 Opposite of hard (4)
10 Short for 'Christmas' (4)
11 Spiky Christmas plant with red berries (5)
13 Money that must be paid to the government (3)
15 Sound made by a sheep (3)

ADVANCED   ⏱ Time ....

Across
4 Poisonous (5)
6 Small jumping insect (4)
7 Cut grass with a machine (3)
9 Someone who studies at university (7)
10 Used for cleaning floors (3)
12 Great anger (4)
13 Damp; slightly wet (5)

Down
1 Carved model of a person or animal (6)
2 Point at a target (3)
3 Flowers growing on a fruit tree (7)
5 Small house in the country (7)
8 Red playing card suit (6)
11 Seed container (3)

Across

1 Small, common flower with white petals and a yellow centre (5)
3 Place where you can buy things (4)
5 Flow of water onto a beach (5)
8 Large, tropical fruit with prickly skin (9)
9 Before second and third (5)
11 Used for keeping money in a shop (4)
12 Shellfish, like a large shrimp (5)

Down

1 Drops of water formed on cool surfaces during the night (3)
2 Speak softly (7)
4 Sheet of glass in a window (4)
6 'Plain' ice cream flavour (7)
7 People who work in an office (5)
8 Some but not all (4)
10 Metal container (3)

Puzzle 133

Across

1 Centre of a wheel (3)
3 Public transport vehicle (3)
5 Used to refer to one or more of something, as in '___ quantity' (3)
7 A waterproof coat (3)
8 All of something (5)
10 Small orange (9)
13 Italian noodles (5)
16 Help (3)
18 Practical joke (3)
19 Pastry dish filled with meat or fruit (3)
20 A Muslim festival (3)

Down

1 Cooked meat from a pig (3)
2 Salted meat from a pig (5)
3 Casual goodbye (3)
4 Female equivalent of 'he' (3)
6 A unit of computer memory storage (4)
9 Video cassette recorder (abbreviation) (1,1,1)
10 Write on a computer keyboard (4)
11 Obtained (3)
12 Picture (5)
14 A small quantity of a drink (3)
15 The length of time that a person has been alive (3)
17 Disc with a film or TV show on it (1,1,1)

Across

1 Nervous; easily frightened (5)
4 Wipe your feet on this (3)
6 Big, hairy spider (9)
7 Long, stringy pasta (9)
10 Substance used to colour hair or clothes (3)
11 Appears when you rub a lamp in some fairy tales (5)

Down

1 Printed words (4)
2 The permanent joining of two adults (8)
3 Opposite of up (4)
4 Very high hill with a peak (8)
5 Meal eaten in the afternoon (3)
7 Opposite of happy (3)
8 The Christmas decorations were ____ on the tree (4)
9 Lazy (4)

Puzzle 135

Across

1 Unusual (8)
5 Paddle used to row a boat (3)
6 Tool used to dig (5)
8 Strong wind which spins everything around (9)
10 Weapon with a long, pointed blade (5)
13 Opposite of high (3)
15 Heavy fall of rain (8)

Down

1 Alien spaceship (1,1,1)
2 The Queen's favourite little dog (5)
3 Details of the roads and land in an area (3)
4 Head movement used to agree (3)
6 Healthy mix of cold, raw vegetables (5)
7 The point where something stops (3)
8 Used to be (3)
9 House made of ice (5)
11 Bundle of soft material (3)
12 Uncooked (3)
14 Time of conflict (3)

Across

1 A person, as distinguished from other animals (5)
3 Hut for storing gardening tools (4)
5 Rest in bed (5)
8 Paper used to cover room walls (9)
9 Underground part of a tree (5)
11 Job that needs to be done (4)
12 Cereal plant used to make flour (5)

Down

1 Male equivalent of 'her' (3)
2 Soap for washing your hair (7)
4 Forest grazing animal with hooves (4)
6 Shadow of the moon against the sun (7)
7 Thin material used for writing on (5)
8 Direction in which the sun sets (4)
10 Rest your bottom on a chair (3)

Puzzle 137

ADVANCED ⏱ Time ....

Across
1 Possesses (3)
3 Knock quickly (3)
5 Christmas song 'The Holly and the ___' (3)
7 Spoil something (3)
8 With nothing inside (5)
10 Holiday for a newly married couple (9)
13 Clothing for your feet (5)
16 Make your skin turn darker in the sun (3)
18 Utilise something (3)
19 Forbid something (3)
20 Opposite of old (3)

Down
1 Sing with closed lips (3)
2 Device that makes a loud warning noise (5)
3 Cereal used in bread and biscuits (3)
4 Fizzy drink (3)
6 Religious song (4)
9 Female parent (3)
10 Say this to ask people to be quiet (4)
11 Large type of deer (3)
12 Frequently (5)
14 Young of a tiger, lion or bear (3)
15 Our closest star (3)
17 At this time (3)

Across
1 Meal at midday (5)
4 Thick blanket for the floor (3)
6 The day before today (9)
7 A letter of the alphabet that isn't a vowel (9)
10 There are five at the end of your foot (3)
11 Wading bird with long thin legs (5)

Down
1 Wife of a Lord (4)
2 Something that makes no sense (8)
3 Rabbit-like fast-running animal (4)
4 Device used to heat a room (8)
5 Statue burnt on Bonfire Night (3)
7 Common family pet (3)
8 Cry of pain (4)
9 Place with houses, shops, offices and buildings (4)

Puzzle 139

Across
4 A ball of ice cream (5)
6 Skin of a fruit or vegetable (4)
7 Which person? (3)
9 Grand house (7)
10 Past tense of 'do', as in 'what I ___ yesterday' (3)
12 Big African wildcat with a shaggy mane (4)
13 Male duck (5)

Down
1 Land surrounded by water (6)
2 Pull one vehicle with another (3)
3 Mythical creature with a woman's body and a fish's tail (7)
5 Ghost (7)
8 Small plant with purple flowers (6)
11 Not wet (3)

Across
1 Identifying piece of paper (5)
3 Boat made for travelling at sea (4)
5 Show off (5)
8 Bird in the pear tree? (9)
9 Animal used for riding (5)
11 Part of a plant that holds it in the ground (4)
12 School subject (5)

Down
1 To throw a ball high (3)
2 Loud noise heard during a storm (7)
4 Piece of paper in a book (4)
6 Juicy fruit, like a small peach (7)
7 Small handheld lamp (5)
8 Look closely at something (4)
10 Short for et cetera; 'and other things like this' (3)

Time

ADVANCED

Time _____

Across

1 Two of these at the entrance to your mouth (4)
4 Thin length of metal used to carry electricity (4)
7 Large hairy monster believed to live in the Himalayas (4)
8 Measure of area for land (4)
9 Not safe (9)
12 Slope (4)
14 Move something away from you (4)
16 Round object used in games (4)
17 Deep breath when you are tired (4)

Down

1 Place something down (3)
2 Seat hung on chains, especially at a play area (5)
3 Long period of history (3)
5 Repeat the same sound again (4)
6 Untidy state (4)
9 Earth; soil (4)
10 Lacking in sensation (4)
11 Response (5)
13 A dog's foot (3)
15 Female bird, such as a chicken (3)

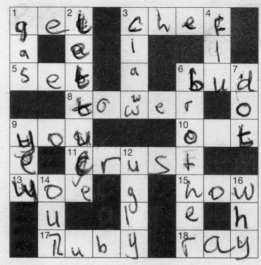

Across

1 A hair-styling product (3)
3 A restaurant cook (4)
5 Adjust a clock or watch (3)
6 Unopened flower (3)
8 Tall, narrow building (5)
9 The person I am talking to (3)
10 Not at home (3)
11 Dry end of a sandwich (5)
13 Misery; misfortune (3)
15 In what way? (3)
17 A red jewel (4)
18 Thin beam of sunlight (3)

Down

1 For example: oxygen or hydrogen (3)
2 Green, leafy vegetable used in salads (7)
3 An animal's sharp, curved nail (4)
4 Illness often caught in the winter (3)
6 Male sibling (7)
7 A small speck (3)
9 An evergreen tree with red berries (3)
12 Not pretty (4)
14 Belonging to us (3)
16 For what reason? (3)

Across

1 For example: rain, snow and wind (7)
6 Short version of 'internet' (3)
7 Ancient Roman language (5)
8 Machine for heating food (9)
10 Big; sizeable (5)
12 Chew food and swallow (3)
13 Scary creature (7)

Down

1 Building with sails turned by the wind (8)
2 Loft (5)
3 Carved pumpkin festival (9)
4 Go bad; decay (3)
5 Family relative born before you (8)
9 A secret spy (5)
11 To crash with force (3)

MICROWAVI

ADVANCED

Time

Across

1 Game played on horseback (4)
3 Big brass instrument (4)
5 Decreased the price (7)
9 Salt water covering a large part of the Earth's surface (3)
10 Cloth used to make jeans (5)
11 Tall tree with broad leaves (3)
12 A series of related tasks (7)
16 Male deer (4)
17 No longer alive (4)

Down

1 Vegetable, looks like a large, yellow carrot (7)
2 The smallest whole number above zero (3)
3 Abbreviation for the day after Wednesday (3)
4 Insect that makes honey (3)
5 Like a TV without pictures (5)
6 Move in time with music (5)
7 Object in sky with bright tail (5)
8 A four-sided shape used on playing cards (7)
13 Deep groove made by wheels (3)
14 Container for liquid, with handle and mouth (3)
15 Large edible sea fish, often served with chips (3)

Level Four:

Ace Puzzlers

Puzzle 145

1		2		3			4		
5						6			7
				8	9				
10						11		12	
			13		14				
15	16						17		18
		19		20					
21							22		
		23			24				
25					26				
		27							

Across

3 Horned farmyard animal (4)

5 Mad (5)

6 Go quickly; hurry (4)

8 List of food in a restaurant (4)

10 Female sheep (3)

11 Pond-dwelling amphibian (4)

13 The unusually long part of a giraffe's body (4)

15 Louse often found in hair (3)

17 TV company, 'British Broadcasting Corporation' (abbreviation) (1,1,1)

19 Opposite of fast (4)

21 The story in a book or film (4)

22 Wonder (3)

23 A little island (4)

25 Unpleasant feeling caused by injury (4)

26 Sound made by a sheep or goat (5)

27 Take hold of something roughly (4)

Down

1 Surface on which films are projected (6)

2 Mother or father (6)

3 Somewhere people go to keep fit (3)

4 Elephant's nose (5)

7 Strike (3)

9 Part of your body used to see (3)

12 The final 'W' in the internet abbreviation WWW (3)

13 Nothing; zero (3)

14 A farmyard animal; a calf's mother (3)

16 Sick; not well (3)

17 Jacket as part of a school uniform (6)

18 Design and make (6)

19 Wound caused by a bee or wasp (5)

20 Nocturnal bird of prey (3)

21 Seed inside an orange (3)

24 The tide's movement away from the land (3)

ACE PUZZLERS

Puzzle 146

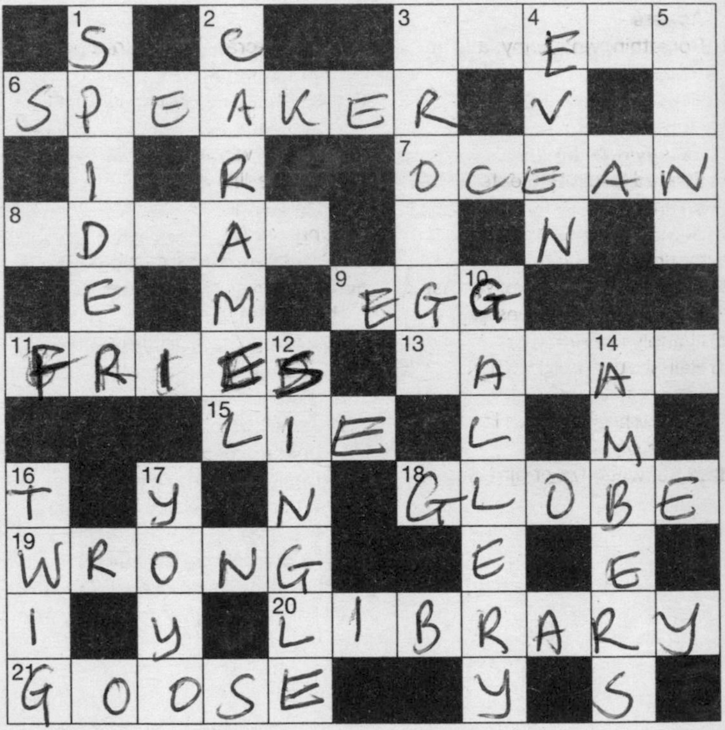

Across

3 Something you enjoy; a reward (5)

6 Person who is talking (7)

7 Huge expanse of water (5)

8 Exactly right (5)

9 Shelled food often eaten fried, scrambled or boiled (3)

11 Snack food often served with hamburgers (5)

13 Light-brown colour, often used when describing eyes (5)

15 Not tell the truth (3)

18 Ball-shaped map of the Earth (5)

19 Incorrect (5)

20 Place where you can borrow books (7)

21 Large, white water bird (5)

Down

1 Creepy-crawly with eight legs (6)

2 Soft toffee (7)

3 Narrow box for animals to eat from (6)

4 Number wholly divisible by '2' (4)

5 Large, edible sea fish (4)

10 Place to display art (7)

12 Only one (6)

14 Glowing remains of a fire (6)

16 Short, thin piece of tree branch (4)

17 Spinning toy on a string (2-2)

Puzzle 147

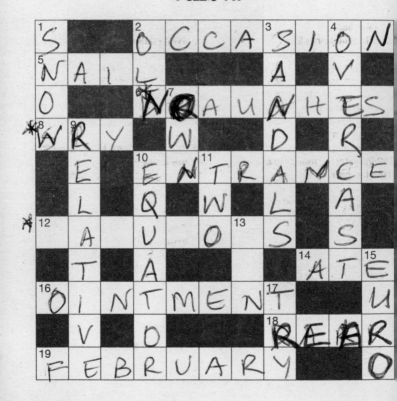

¹S		²O	C	C	A	³S	I	⁴O		N
⁵N	A	I	L			A		V		
O		⁶L	⁷N	A	U	N	H	E	S	
⁸W	⁹R	Y		W		D		R		
	E		¹⁰E	N	¹¹T	R	A	N	C	E
	L		Q		W		L		A	
¹²		U			O		S		A	
	A		Á			¹³		¹⁴A	T	¹⁵E
¹⁶O	I	N	T	M	E	N	¹⁷T			U
	V		O				¹⁸R	E	A	R
¹⁹F	E	B	R	U	A	R	Y			O

Across

2 Special event (8)
5 Hard part at the end of your finger (4)
6 Game with black tiles decorated with white dots representing numbers (8)
8 Slightly mocking, as in 'a ___ smile' (3)
10 The way in to a place (8)
12 Wonderful; marvellous (8)
14 Had some food (3)
16 Cream used for healing skin (8)
18 Back part of something (4)
19 Second month (8)

Down

1 White flakes that fall from the sky (4)
2 Advanced in years (3)
3 Summer shoes (7)
4 Cloudy (8)
7 Possess (3)
9 Someone belonging to the same family (8)
10 The ring around the middle of the Earth (7)
11 An even number just less than three (3)
13 A very big vase (3)
15 Currency used in some parts of Europe (4)
17 Attempt (3)

ACE PUZZLERS

Puzzle 148

1 K	O	2 A	L	3 A	■	■	4 G	A	5 A	P
E	■	L	■	6 C	7 A	L	L	■	L	■
8 T	R	A	V	E	L	■	9 A	G	O	■
C	■	R	■	■	S	■	S	■	N	■
10 H	E	M	■	11 T	O	12 A	S	T	E	13 R
U	■	■	■	I	■	C	■	■	■	E
14 P	15 R	E	16 S	E	17 N	T	■	18 P	A	L
■	I	■	T	■	O	■	■	R	■	E
■	19 V	D	U	■	20 S	21 A	M	D	S	A
■	E	■	22 D		E	L	■	U	■	S
23 X	R	A	Y	■	■	24 L	A	D	E	E

Ketchup

Across

1. Furry Australian animal that eats eucalyptus leaves (5)
4. Tiny, biting fly (4)
6. Shout out a name (4)
8. Go from one place to another (6)
9. Once upon a time, a long time ___ (3)
10. Folded and sewn edge of cloth (3)
11. Device for browning bread (7)
14. The here and now (7)
18. Friend (3)
19. Visual display unit (abbreviation) (1,1,1)
20. Crispy pastry case filled with Indian meat or vegetables (6)
22. Fight between two people (4)
23. Photograph taken of the inside of the body (1-3)
24. Deep spoon with long handle, often used to serve soup (5)

Down

1. Tomato sauce (7)
2. Wakes you in the morning (5)
3. Playing card '1' (3)
4. Clear container for drinking from (5)
5. On your own; by yourself (5)
7. This as well; too (4)
11. Make a knot in a strip of material (3)
12. Perform on stage (3)
13. Let go; set free (7)
15. Stream (5)
16. Learn about something (5)
17. The part of the face used for smelling (4)
18. Pleased with yourself for doing well (5)
21. Everyone (3)

Puzzle 149

Across

1. Not a lie (5)
4. Very cold (3)
6. Black liquid fuel extracted from the ground (3)
8. Italian food made of layers of meat and pasta (7)
9. Weapon that fires bullets (3)
10. A single leaf of a flower (5)
12. Precious stone (3)
14. A small hotel (3)
15. Not on (3)
17. No longer a child (5)
20. The blackened remains of a fire (3)
21. Bird chirping noise (7)
22. Urgent call for help (abbreviation) (1,1,1)
23. Make a mistake (3)
24. Doctor's assistant (5)

Down

1. Bright spring flower that grows from a bulb (5)
2. Knock over or tip (5)
3. A brightly-coloured pen used to colour over important words (11)
4. The ability to think up new ideas (11)
5. Not old (5)
7. Machine for weaving cloth (4)
11. Small mischievous fairy (3)
13. Snake-shaped fish (3)
15. Cereal plant used for food (4)
16. Incorrect; untrue (5)
18. Say something clearly (5)
19. Number of corners on a triangle (5)

Puzzle 150

Across

2 Car with driver available for hire (4)
4 Run very fast (6)
6 For example: parsley, sage or thyme (4)
8 Scented flower with a thorny stem (4)
10 What we breathe (3)
11 Tool used to tighten bolts (7)
13 Circus entertainer who leaps around (7)
16 You have two of these to listen to things (3)
17 Not able to speak (4)
18 Lump in a piece of string or rope (4)
20 Hard hat used to protect the head (6)
21 Period of twelve months (4)

Down

1 Green lawn plant (5)
2 Thick black liquid used for surfacing roads (3)
3 A food item needed for a recipe (10)
4 A red fruit with seeds on the outside (10)
5 Opposite of fat (4)
7 A metal pole (3)
9 Long story, for example 'The Odyssey' (4)
12 School test (4)
13 Noah's ship for pairs of animals (3)
14 Solemn promise (4)
15 Stomach (5)
19 And not, as in 'neither this nor that' (3)

Puzzle 151

Across

2 Crunchy green or red fruit (5)
5 Hole in the nose (7)
7 Fish's eggs (3)
8 Sprint (3)
10 Small water turtle (8)
11 Creamy frozen dessert (3,5)
13 Large, Australian, flightless bird (3)
14 Going through; stopping at (3)
15 Red edible shellfish with two big claws (7)
16 Left over; not used (5)

Down

1 Make loud noises while you sleep (5)
2 Letters arranged in order (8)
3 The place where British laws are made (10)
4 The night before a big day, such as Christmas (3)
6 Father Christmas (5,5)
9 Vehicle with three wheels (8)
12 Someone who protects a place (5)
14 Solemn promise (3)

Puzzle 152

Across

3 Stumble over something (4)
5 Large stringed instrument (5)
6 Parent's sister (4)
8 Not closed (4)
10 A donkey (3)
11 Challenge someone to do something (4)
13 Settee (4)
15 Discard something unwanted (3)
17 Small, crawling insect (3)
19 Edge of something (4)
21 Pimple (4)
22 Common road vehicle (3)
23 Concept (4)
25 Selfish; not generous (4)
26 Push a computer key (5)
27 Joint where your leg bends (4)

Down

1 Long cake filled with cream and topped with chocolate (6)
2 Opposite of open (6)
3 Also; as well (3)
4 Black and white bear-like animal found in China (5)
7 Abbreviation for the day after Monday (3)
9 Please turn over (abbreviation) (1,1,1)
12 Was in charge (3)
13 A long metal shoe worn for a winter sport (3)
14 Enemy (3)
16 Mischievous pixie (3)
17 Someone who shoots arrows at a target (6)
18 A common songbird (6)
19 Very unpleasant smell (5)
20 Stop living (3)
21 The total amount (3)
24 Large monkey without a tail (3)

Puzzle 153

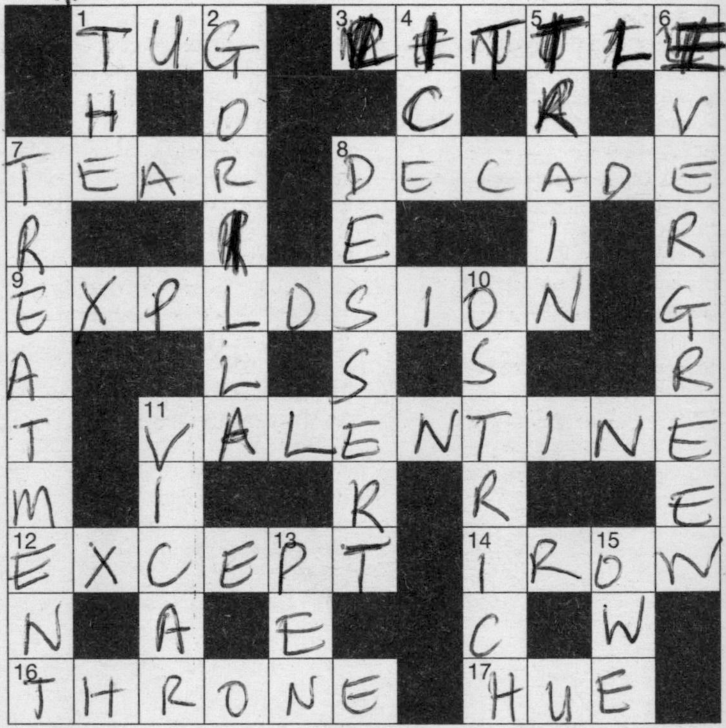

Time .... **ACE PUZZLERS**

Across

1 Powerful boat used for pulling ships (3)

3 Small (6)

7 Drop of water from your eye (4)

8 A period of ten years (6)

9 Result of a bomb going off (9)

11 Card sent to someone you love (9)

12 Other than, as in 'I want them all, _ _ _ _ _ _ for that' (6)

14 Remove creases from clothing (4)

16 Special chair for a king or queen (6)

17 Tint; colour (3)

Down

1 Definite article; a particular item, as in 'I want ___ one over there' (3)

2 Large African ape (7)

4 Frozen water (3)

5 Railway vehicle (5)

6 Tree that stays green all year long (9)

7 Medical care (9)

8 Sweet course of a meal (7)

10 Large bird known to sometimes bury its head in the sand (7)

11 Priest (5)

13 Used for writing with ink (3)

15 Need to pay something back (3)

Answers

Beginners

1

B		S		U
L	E	M	O	N
I		A		D
N	U	R	S	E
D		T		R

2

	F	A	W	N
	E		H	
S	N	A	I	L
	C		S	
W	E	A	K	

3

S	H	A	P	E
	O		R	
G	R	A	I	N
	S		Z	
N	E	V	E	R

4

C	H	E	F	
	E		L	
M	A	J	O	R
	R		U	
	T	I	R	E

5

R	O	P	E	
U		I		P
B	L	A	D	E
Y		N		A
	L	O	C	K

6

	L	A	M	P
	N		O	
S	I	G	H	T
O		E		
W	I	L	D	

7

S		J	O	G
T		O		E
A	L	I	E	N
F		N		I
F	A	T	E	

8

S	T	A	R	
	R		U	
T	A	B	L	E
	M		E	
	P	A	R	K

9

	P	I	C	K
	E		A	
S	T	O	N	E
	A		D	
P	L	A	Y	

10
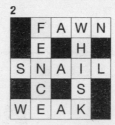

	L	A	M	B
	M		O	
L	O	B	B	Y
A		E		
G	I	R	L	

11

S	N	A	C	K
	O		H	
V	I	D	E	O
	S		A	
T	E	N	T	H

12

H	U	B		S
O		L	I	T
B		U		A
B	Y	E		I
Y		S	U	N

13

B		P	A	D
R		U		R
A	P	P	L	E
S		P		S
S	L	Y		S

14

	S	W	I	M
		A		A
J	O	L	L	Y
O		L		
B	U	S	Y	

15

L	U	C	K	
I		A		L
F	A	B	L	E
T		L		A
	M	E	N	D

16

H	A	D		A
E		R	U	B
A		I		B
V	A	N		E
Y		K	E	Y

17

	S	I	G	N
	M		R	
W	I	P	E	R
	L		E	
W	E	E	K	

18

C	A	R	D	
	C		U	
S	O	L	V	E
	R		E	
	N	O	T	E

19

	C	A	L	F
		R		U
T	I	G	E	R
E		U		
D	E	E	P	

20

G	Y	M		F
L		O	N	E
O		U		A
V	E	T		S
E		H	U	T

21

P	E	R	C	H
	R		O	
T	R	A	C	E
	O		O	
C	R	E	A	M

22

P	A	S	S	
	M		W	
M	A	G	I	C
	Z		N	
	E	V	E	N

23

	S	A	V	E
	M		E	
P	E	N	N	Y
	L		O	
S	L	I	M	

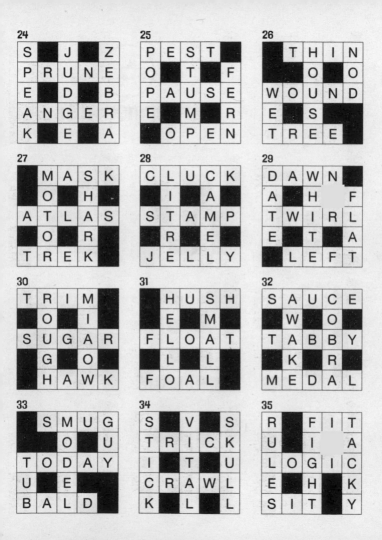

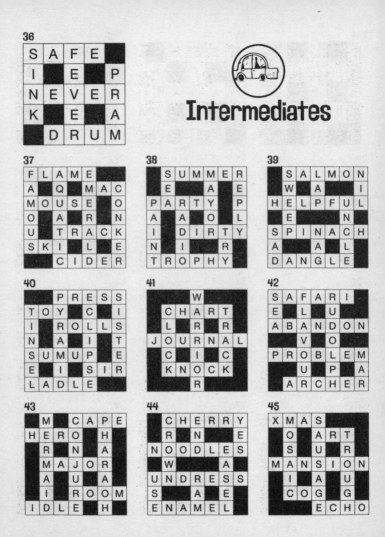

36

```
S A F E .
I . E . P
N E V E R
K . E . A
. D R U M
```

Intermediates

37

```
. F L A M E
A . Q . M A C
M O U S E . O
O . A . R . N
U . T R A C K
S K I . L . E
. . C I D E R
```

38

```
. S U M M E R
. E . A . E
P A R T Y . P
A . A . O . L
I . D I R T Y
N . I . R
T R O P H Y
```

39

```
. S A L M O N
. W . A . . I
H E L P F U L
. E . . . N
S P I N A C H
A . . A . L
D A N G L E
```

40

```
. P R E S S
T O Y . C . I
I . R O L L S
N . A . I . T
S U M U P . E
E . I . S I R
L A D L E
```

41

```
. . . W
. C H A R T
. L . R . R
J O U R N A L
. C . I . C
. K N O C K
. . . R
```

42

```
S A F A R I
E . L . U
A B A N D O N
. V . O
P R O B L E M
. U . P . A
A R C H E R
```

43

```
. M . C A P E
H E R O . H
R . N . A
. M A J O R
A . U . A
I . R O O M
I D L E . H
```

44

```
. C H E R R Y
. R . N . E
N O O D L E S
. W . A
U N D R E S S
S . . A . E
E N A M E L
```

45

```
X M A S .
O . A R T
S . U . R
M A N S I O N
I . A . U
C O G . G
. . E C H O
```

46

```
. . L . . . .
. W H E A T .
. O . T . R .
B R O T H E R
. R . U . A .
. Y A C H T .
. . . E . . .
```

47

```
. H . S . I .
T A D P O L E
. R . I . L .
S P A N N E R
. O . A . G .
C O N C E A L
. N . H . L .
```

48

```
. C . A C R E
F O O D . E .
. L . D . F .
. L A R G E .
. A . E . R .
. G . S E E D
L E N S . E .
```

49

```
P L U M E . .
L . N . V O W
A L I V E . A
G . C . N . L
U . O N I O N
E A R . N . U
. . N I G H T
```

50

```
. V E R M I N
. I . A . A .
S A T I N . S
H . A . O . T
A . B E R R Y
R . L . A . A
P R E T T Y .
```

51

```
. W I N T E R
. R . O . Y .
M I S T A K E
. T . . . N .
W E L L I E S
A . . O . E .
S Y M B O L .
```

52

```
. C O S M I C
. L . I . U .
C O M P O S E
. W . . . C .
U N U S U A L
F . . U . R .
O R A N G E .
```

53

```
D U S K . . .
I . P . S I R
S C O O P . E
C . O . R . M
U . K N I F E
S A Y . N . D
. . . U G L Y
```

54

```
. . Q U A C K
. . F . N . A
P A T I E N T
. . L . F . C
S C O O T E R
. . O . R . L
G N O M E . .
```

55

```
. . M . . C .
. C A M E R A
F O R . . A .
. M E S S Y .
. M . . H O G
C O U P O N .
. N . . . E .
```

56

```
. K . D I E T
L A C E . X .
. R . F . C .
. A P R I L .
. O . O . A .
. K . S O I L
Z E S T . M .
```

57

```
. F O S S I L
. E . O . U .
J E W E L . N
E . A . V . C
A . F R E S H
N . E . A . .
S O R R O W .
```

58

```
H A R P . .
. B . R I P
. S . E . R
P O S T M A N
. R . E . Y
. B I N . E
. . D A R E
```

59

```
. L . S . G
V E H I C L E
. T . L . A
S T R E T C H
. E . N . I
C R A C K E R
. S . E . R
```

60

```
. . D . . S
. P O L I C E
M U M . . R
. P E A C E
. P . . L A X
H E L I U M
. T . . B
```

61

```
. . S P I N E
. C . A . E
T H U N D E R
. U . C . D
T R E A C L E
. C . K . E
S H E E P
```

62

```
. . . V . .
. G I A N T
. R . M . E
C O M P L E X
. O . I . T
. M A R C H
. E
```

63

```
G A T E A U
U . R . T
T E A C H E R
. . C . L
A C T R E S S
. . O . T . A
. F R I E N D
```

64

```
. F A M O U S
E . E . . O
S T A T I O N
. C . . C
W H I S P E R
E . A . A
D R A G O N
```

65

```
J . B E E F
P A I R . M
N . I . E
U T T E R .
A . I . A
R . S A L T
M Y T H . D
```

66

```
. F A T H E R
. L . O . E
S U G A R . P
T . R . S . L
R . E V E R Y
A . E . . O
W I N D O W
```

67

```
. . C . . .
. E R A S E
. M . R . A
C A V A L R Y
. I . V . T
. L E A S H
. . N
```

68

```
. D . F . S
T O N I G H T
. O . Z . A
D R I Z Z L E
. . M . L
R A I N B O W
. T . G . W
```

69

```
. P . S I G N
P A T H . A
. N . U . R
. T O T A L
. H . T . A
. E . L U N G
T R E E . D
```

70

```
. P R O M P T
. I . . A . O
H E A V Y . A
A . W . O . S
P . F I R S T
P . U . . O .
Y E L L O W
```

71

```
. . T . . D
. C A R P E T
F O X . . S .
. P I X I E .
. P . . D R Y
S E C R E T .
. R . . A
```

72

```
R E C I P E .
A . O . R .
W E L C O M E
. . L . M .
S P E C I A L
. . G . S . A
. C E L E R Y
```

73

```
C O P E . .
O . L . B Y E
L L A M A . A
U . N . R . R
M . E L B O W
N U T . E . I
. . D R A G
```

74

```
. U P S E T
. P . A . A
T O U R I S T
. L . A . T
G L A S S E S
. E . O . R
A N G L E
```

75

```
. . W . . I
. M A R I N E
F A N . . S .
. S T A G E .
. T . . I C Y
D E P A R T .
. R . . L
```

76

```
. . S
. W H E E L
. I . R . A
A N T I Q U E
. D . O . G
. Y O U T H
. . S
```

77

```
. F R E N C H
. L . G . A
G O G G L E S
. O . . N .
P R O B L E M
I . . O . M
N O B O D Y
```

78

```
S P O T .
. I . H I P
C . I . A
U N D R E S S
I . S . T
C U T . E
. . Y O L K
```

79

```
V A S E .
A . H . B A T
C H I N A . U
U . E . D . R
U . L I G H T
M I D . E . L
. . F R E E
```

80

```
. E M P T Y
. P . U . I
P R E S E N T
. I . T . S
R E L A T E D
. S . R . L
S T U D Y
```

81

```
. C . T R I M
F A I R . L
. G . A . L
. O N I O N
. U . N . E
. L . E A S T
D E E R . S
```

82

```
V I N E . . .
. N . C A N .
. J . S . O .
V U L T U R E
. R . A . M .
. Y E S . A .
. . . Y E L L
```

83

```
. . . . C . .
. C H E S S .
. L . N . T .
D E S T R O Y
. A . U . N .
. N U R S E .
. Y . . . . .
```

84

```
T U R K E Y .
A . E . N . .
P E L I C A N
. . E . H . .
P H A R A O H
. S . N . . E
. L E T T E R
```

85

```
. D . S W I M
D E E P . L .
. S . I . L .
. S E N S E .
. E . A . G .
. R . C O A L
I T C H . L .
```

86

```
P L O T . . .
. I . O W E .
. Z . D . N .
H A N D B A G
. R . L . M .
. D U E . E .
. . . R O L L
```

87

```
. . . H . . .
. S T O R M .
. H . R . O .
V A L I A N T
. P . Z . E .
. E B O N Y .
. . . N . . .
```

88

	H		S		D	
R	E	F	E	R	E	E
	X		A		S	
N	A	U	G	H	T	Y
	G		U		I	
G	O	S	L	I	N	G
	N		L		Y	

89

	S		F	I	L	M
S	T	I	R		U	
	R		E		L	
	E	X	C	E	L	
	T		K		A	
	C		L	O	B	E
S	H	O	E		Y	

90

	A	B	O	A	R	D
	I		R			A
A	M	U	S	E		I
D		N		N		R
U		D	I	A	R	Y
L		E		U		
T	A	R	T	A	N	

91

	A	R	C	T	I	C
	L		A			A
F	L	O	R	I	S	T
	E			T		
P	Y	J	A	M	A	S
I			I		I	
G	A	R	D	E	N	

92

		S	P	E	A	K
S	E	A		P		E
T			P	A	I	N	T
R		L		S		T
I	D	I	O	T		L
K		N		L	I	E
E	A	G	L	E		

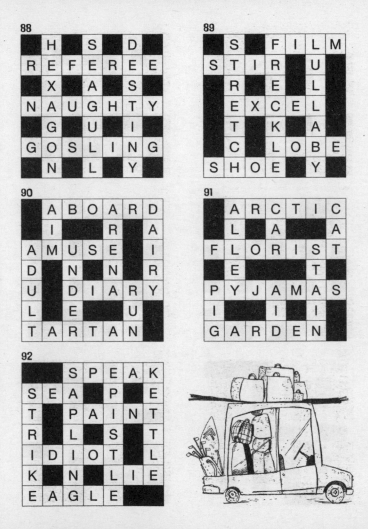

Advanced

93

N	O	V	E	M	B	E	R	
O		I		A		A	
W	A	X		M	A	N	G	O
		E		A			N
C	O	N	S	T	A	B	L	E
A			C		A		
P	E	A	C	H		N	I	P
	I		O		J		E
	D	O	W	N	P	O	U	R

94

		G			A		
	C		A	L	A	R	M
P	O	E	M			M	O	B
	N		B		M		R
	V	I	L	L	A	I	N
	I		E		L		I
A	C	E			L	E	N	S
	T	R	A	C	E		G
	R				T		

95

E	N	J	O	Y		T	
L					R	O	O	F
F	L	O	A	T		R		A
		S		R		N		C
A	S	T	R	O	N	A	U	T
U		R		U		D	
N		I		T	H	O	R	N
T	I	C	K					E
		H		Q	U	I	E	T

96

W	A	T	E	R			
E		O		A		B	O	W
E		B		C		A		A
P	R	O	F	E	S	S	O	R
		G			E		
V	E	G	E	T	A	B	L	E
I		A		R		A		D
P	U	N		I		L		I
			P	I	L	O	T

97

B	U	T		T	R	U	E	
U		E		R			M	
G	U	M		I		C	U	P
		P	H	O	T	O		I
A	G	E				N	A	P
S		S	T	I	F	F		
H	O	T		S		I	V	Y
	U			L		R		E
	T	A	L	E		M	A	T

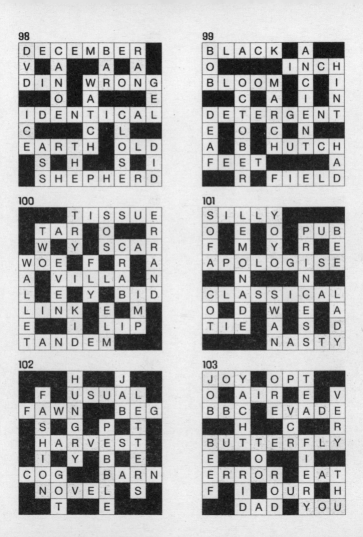

98

```
D E C E M B E R ·
V · A · · A · A
D I N · W R O N G
· · O · A · · E
I D E N T I C A L
C · · C · L · ·
E A R T H · O L D
· S · H · · S · I
· S H E P H E R D
```

99

```
B L A C K · A ·
O · · · I N C H
B L O O M · C · I
· · C · A · I · N
D E T E R G E N T
E · O · C · N ·
A · B · H U T C H
F E E T · · · A
· · R · F I E L D
```

100

```
· · · T I S S U E
· T A R · O · · R
· W · Y · S C A R
W O E · F · R · A
A · V I L L A · N
L · E · Y · B I D
L I N K · E · M
E · · I · L I P
T A N D E M
```

101

```
S I L L Y · · ·
O · E · O · P U B
F · M · Y · R · E
A P O L O G I S E
· · N · · N ·
C L A S S I C A L
O · D · W · E · A
T I E · A · S · D
· · N A S T Y
```

102

```
· · H · · J
· F · U S U A L
F A W N · · B E G
· S · G · P · T
· H A R V E S T
· I · Y · B · E
C O G · · B A R N
· N O V E L · S
· · T · · E
```

103

```
J O Y · O P T
O · A I R · E · V
B B C · E V A D E
· · H · · C · R
B U T T E R F L Y
E · O · · I
E R R O R · E A T
F · I · O U R · H
· D A D · Y O U
```

104

```
. . . V I E W .
E . D I E . O .
M O O . S . I N K
B . O F T E N . E
E N D . . S U N .
R . L I T R E . N
S U E . E . R O E
. . R . S E T . .
. N E W T . . . .
```

105

```
H E A R T . V .
I . . . S O U P
S C A R F . L . U
. . I . L . C . R
M A R M A L A D E
O . P . S . N . .
A . O . K N O C K
T I R E . . . . E
. . T . I V O R Y
```

106

```
S H A M E F U L .
I . L . . E . U .
N U T . N E I G H
. . A . O . . . O
H U R R I C A N E
O . . S . G . . .
W H O L E . A C T
. U . O . . I . U
. E N T R A N C E
```

107

```
M U R A L . . . .
E . O . I . T I P
S . M . K . O . A
S C A R E C R O W
. . N . . . T . .
A F T E R N O O N
W . I . O . I . E
E T C . O . S . S
. . . T H E F T .
```

108

```
. . S . . B . .
. L . A T T I C
L E A F . . T O Y
. O . A . A . M .
. P A R S N I P .
. A . I . C . O .
A R K . . H I S S
. D I S C O . T .
. . N . . R . . .
```

109

```
B I R C H . T .
A . . . . W R A P
D R E S S . E . E
. . M . T . M . A
S E P T E M B E R
O . E . A . L . .
A . R . K N E E L
P R O D . . . . E
. . R . F R O S T
```

110

I	R	I	S	■	A	■	■	■
L	■	■	P	I	N	E	■	C
L	I	M	E	■	T	U	N	E
■	■	■	E	■	R	■	L	■
T	O	A	D	S	T	O	O	L
A	■	L	■	R	■	■	■	■
M	I	S	S	■	A	C	R	E
E	■	O	A	T	S	■	■	Y
■	■	W	■	H	O	L	E	■

111

P	A	T	T	E	R	N	■	■
H	■	A	■	S	■	O	■	C
E	E	L	■	C	A	R	O	L
A	■	O	■	A	■	■	■	A
S	U	N	F	L	O	W	E	R
A	■	■	A	■	A	■	■	I
N	I	G	H	T	■	S	O	N
T	■	A	■	O	■	T	■	E
■	■	S	E	R	P	E	N	T

112

O	P	E	R	A	■	S	■	■
F	■	■	■	■	T	A	U	T
F	L	A	S	H	■	T	■	R
■	■	I	■	Y	■	C	■	E
H	O	R	S	E	S	H	O	E
E	■	M	■	N	■	E	■	■
L	■	A	■	A	L	L	O	W
P	A	I	L	■	■	■	■	I
■	■	L	■	G	R	E	E	N

113

S	L	O	W	■	K	■	■	■
A	■	■	O	P	E	N	■	Y
P	A	I	R	■	G	A	M	E
■	■	■	L	■	M	■	■	A
T	E	D	D	Y	B	E	A	R
A	■	O	■	■	A	■	■	■
R	O	O	M	■	K	I	N	G
T	■	R	U	L	E	■	■	U
■	■	G	■	R	A	F	T	■

114

■	■	E	■	■	N	■	■	■
■	C	■	M	U	S	I	C	■
D	A	M	P	■	■	B	E	T
■	L	■	I	■	W	■	N	■
■	C	U	R	R	A	N	T	■
■	I	■	E	■	I	■	U	■
C	U	T	■	■	T	U	R	N
■	M	O	V	I	E	■	Y	■
■	■	N	■	■	R	■	■	■

115

H	O	M	E	W	O	R	K	■
A	■	A	■	■	W	■	I	■
T	A	G	■	C	L	O	T	H
■	■	I	■	Y	■	■	■	E
D	E	C	K	C	H	A	I	R
O	■	■	■	L	■	D	■	■
G	R	A	P	E	■	D	A	M
■	■	O	■	A	■	E	■	A
W	O	N	D	E	R	E	D	■

116

```
D W A R F . C . .
I . . . . H O O F
M E D I A . L . O
. . O . G . L . U
P O L A R B E A R
U . P . E . C . .
L . H . E X T R A
L A I R . . . . L
. N . T O W E L .
```

117

```
. . . D O D G E M
. A P E . I . . I
. G . N . P L U S
H O P . C . A . E
A . A P R O N . R
M . S . Y . D I Y
M U S T . O . C .
E . . A . W A Y .
R I B B O N . . .
```

118

```
. . S . . F .
. B . P A N I C
F O I L . B O X
. O . A . P . L
. K E S T R E L
. L . H . I . A
S E W . . S I G N
. T O R S O . E
. . K . N
```

119

```
A J A R . S M O G
N . . A . O . I
T . S T U B B L E
L A W . P . E . V
E . E A S E L . E
R . A . E . C A N
S C R A T C H . I
. U . N . O . N
F E E D . P L U G
```

120

```
F I N C H . F .
E . . . C L A P
W H E E L . A . O
. Y . O . V . N
E V E R Y B O D Y
X . L . A . U .
I . A . L O R R Y
T U S K . . . A
. H . Q U I C K
```

121

```
S C A B . C . .
U . . L O A F . B
M A N E . B L U E
. . . N . . I . A
S A N D P A P E R
I . O . . N . .
D A T E . K E E P
E . E V I L . . U
. . E . E A S T
```

122

```
. . P A S T E L
. F A R . A . A
. O . Y . T R A P
F R O . Z . I . T
L . B R O W N . O
O . O . O . G A P
W E E D . J . S .
E . . A . O A K .
R A B B I T . . .
```

123

```
. . . L . . Y . .
. W . A T L A S .
T H A W . . M E T
I . Y . C . . A .
S H E R I F F . .
K . R . R . . O .
L E D . . C O O P
R O Y A L . . D .
. E . . . E . . .
```

124

```
J A M . L A B . .
A . A R E . O . L
W A N . G L O R Y
. . O . O . . R .
A E R O P L A N E
C . D . . L . . .
H A N D Y . T U B
E . U . A X E . E
. N I P . R E D .
```

125

```
F R E S H . . . .
I . L . E . F E D
R . E . R . L . U
E S P I O N A G E
. . H . . M . . .
B L A C K B I R D
I . N . I . N . I
G E T . S . G . E
. . . S H O R T .
```

126

```
M A R Z I P A N .
A . I . E . O . .
N A G . S A N T A
. H . U . . . D .
A T T E M P T E D
P . . U . O . . .
T R A M P . T O P
. O . E . A . E .
. B U N G A L O W
```

127

```
. . C . . A . . .
. G . A W A R D .
C L A M . T E N .
I . E . T . V . .
. T O R N A D O .
T . A . N . T . .
P E R . G L E E .
R U R A L . D . .
. B . . E . . . .
```

128

A	L	B	U	M		W	
R					L	A	M	P
M	I	N	U	S		R		L
		U		O	R		A
C	O	M	M	U	N	I	T	Y
A		B		N		O	
L		E		D	I	R	T	Y
F	A	R	M				E
		S		S	H	E	E	T

129

T	E	E	T	H		
O		N		A		L	O	G
Y		O		R		O		O
S	C	R	A	M	B	L	E	D
		M				L
F	O	O	T	P	R	I	N	T
R		U		R		P		O
Y	E	S		O		O		I
			P	U	P	I	L

130

S	I	G	H		K	
E		E	D	I	T		O
E	A	R	L		D	R	U	G
		L			I		R
S	A	X	O	P	H	O	N	E
O		M		O		
F	L	A	T		L	A	M	B
T		S	A	I	L		A
		X		Y	O	G	A

131

			S		A	
	B		T	O	X	I	C
F	L	E	A		M	O	W
	O		T		H		T
	S	T	U	D	E	N	T
	S		E		A		A
M	O	P		R	A	G	E
M	O	I	S	T		E
	D		S

132

D	A	I	S	Y		W	
E				S	H	O	P
W	A	V	E	S		I		A
	A		T		S		N
P	I	N	E	A	P	P	L	E
A		I		F		E	
R		L		F	I	R	S	T
T	I	L	L				I
	A		P	R	A	W	N

133

H	U	B		B	U	S	
A		A	N	Y		H		B
M	A	C		E	V	E	R	Y
	O		C		T
T	A	N	G	E	R	I	N	E
Y		O		M	
P	A	S	T	A		A	I	D
E		I		G	A	G		V
	P	I	E		E	I	D

134

```
T I M I D . . .
E . A . O . M A T
X . R . W . O . E
T A R A N T U L A
. . I . . . N . .
S P A G H E T T I
A . G . U . A . D
D Y E . N . I . L
. . . . G E N I E
```

135

```
U N C O M ...
F . O . . A
O A R . S P A...
. . G . A
W H I R L W I N...
A . . A . G
S W O R D . L O W
. A . A . . O . A
D O W N P O U R
```

136

```
H U M A N . S
I . . . . S H E D
S L E E P . A . E
. . C . A . M . E
W A L L P A P E R
E . I . E . O
S . P . R O O T S
T A S K . . . . I
. . E . W H E A T
```

137

```
H A S . R A P
U . I V Y . O . H
M A R . E M P T Y
. E . . U . . . M
H O N E Y M O O N
U . L . . F
S O C K S . T A N
H . U . U S E . O
. B A N . N E W
```

138

```
L U N C H
A . O . A . R U G
D . N . R . A . U
Y E S T E R D A Y
. . E . . . I
C O N S O N A N T
A . S . U . T . O
T O E . C . O . W
. . . H E R O N
```

139

```
. . . I . . T
. M . S C O O P
P E E L . . W H O
. R . A . V . A
. M A N S I O N
. A . D . O . T
D I D . . L I O N
. . D R A K E . M
. . Y . . T
```

141

142

143

144

Ace Puzzlers

145

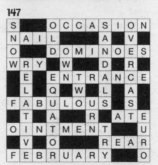

```
S  P     G  O  A  T           
C  R  A  Z  Y        R  U  S  H
R     R     M  E  N  U        I
E  W  E        Y     N  E  W  T
E     N     N  E  C  K     E   
N  I  T     I     O     B  B  C
   L     S  L  O  W     L     R
P  L  O  T     W        A  W  E
I        I  S  L  E     Z     A
P  A  I  N        B  L  E  A  T
      G  R  A  B     R     E   
```

146

```
   S  C        T  R  E  A  T
S  P  E  A  K  E  R     V  U
   I  R        O  C  E  A  N
I  D  E  A  L     U     N  A
   E  M     E  G  G         
F  R  I  E  S     H  A  Z  E  L
      L  I  E        L     M
T  Y     N     G  L  O  B  E
W  R  O  N  G        E     E
I     Y     L  I  B  R  A  R  Y
G  O  O  S  E        Y     S
```

147

```
S        O  C  C  A  S  I  O  N
N  A  I  L        A     V     
O        D  O  M  I  N  O  E  S
W  R  Y     W     D     R     
   E     E  N  T  R  A  N  C  E
   L     Q     W     L     A
F  A  B  U  L  O  U  S     S
   T     A     R     A  T  E
O  I  N  T  M  E  N  T     U
   V     O        R  E  A  R
F  E  B  R  U  A  R  Y     O
```

148

```
K  O  A  L  A        G  N  A  T
E     L     C  A  L  L     L   
T  R  A  V  E  L     A  G  O
C     R     S     S     N
H  E  M     T  O  A  S  T  E  R
U        I     C        E
P  R  E  S  E  N  T     P  A  L
   I     T     O     R     E
   V  D  U     S  A  M  O  S  A
   E     D  U  E  L     U     S
X  R  A  Y        L  A  D  L  E
```

149

```
T  R  U  T  H     I  C  Y
U     P     I     M     O  I  L
L  A  S  A  G  N  A     U     O
I     E     H     G  U  N     O
P  E  T  A  L        I     G  E  M
   L     I  N  N        E
O  F  F     G     A  D  U  L  T
A     A  S  H     T     T     H
T     L     T  W  I  T  T  E  R
S  O  S     E        O     E  E
      E  R  R     N  U  R  S  E
```

150

| | G | | | | T | A | X | I |
|S|P|R|I|N|T| |A| |N|
|T| |A| |H|E|R|B| |G|
R	O	S	E		I			A	I	R
A			S	P	A	N	N	E	R		E
W		I					X		D
B		A	C	R	O	B	A	T		I
E	A	R		A		M	U	T	E
R		K	N	O	T		M		N
R		O		H	E	L	M	E	T
Y	E	A	R				Y

151

S					A	P	P	L	E
N	O	S	T	R	I	L		A		V
O		A			P		R	O	E
R	U	N		T		H		L		E
E		T	E	R	R	A	P	I	N
		A		I		B		A
	I	C	E	C	R	E	A	M		G
	L		Y		T		E	M	U
V	I	A		C					A
O		U		L	O	B	S	T	E	R
W	A	S	T	E					D

152

|E| |C| |T|R|I|P|
C	E	L	L	O			A	U	N	T
L		O			O	P	E	N		U
A	S	S			T		D	A	R	E
I		E		S	O	F	A		A
R	I	D		K		O		A	N	T
	M		S	I	D	E	R		H
S	P	O	T		I		C	A	R
U			I	D	E	A		H		U
M	E	A	N			P	R	E	S	S
		K	N	E	E		R		H

153

	T	U	G		L	I	T	T	L	E
	H		O		C		R		V
T	E	A	R		D	E	C	A	D	E
R		I		E		I			R
E	X	P	L	O	S	I	O	N		R
A		L		S		S			G
T		V	A	L	E	N	T	I	N	E
M		I		R		R			E
E	X	C	E	P	T		I	R	O	N
N		A		E			C		W
T	H	R	O	N	E		H	U	E